BUSINESS INTELLIGENCE & SCIENTIFIC MANAGEMENT TRAINING

Translated from Romanian book:

"CURS DE SAH SI MANAGEMENT STIINTIFIC"

Copyright © 2014 Constantin V. Mihaescu

All rights reserved

ISBN-13: 978-1502558275

Copyright © 2014 Constantin V. Mihaescu

All rights reserved

ISBN-13: 978-1515034148

ISBN-10: 1515034143

CONSTANTIN MIHAESCU

BUSINESS INTELLIGENCE & SCIENTIFIC MANAGEMENT TRAINING

Business Management Manual Using Scientific Chess vs. Computer, Chess Online and Instructive Pictured Chess Games. How to Play Chess Faster and Win

CreateSpace Publishing

US-WA-Seattle, 2015

www.createspace.com

Dedicated to the memory

of my dear father

Victor

Table of Contents

Part three – THE SCIENTIFIC STUDY OF CHESS GAMES AGAINST COMPUTER

Acknowledgments

I am extremely grateful to Transilvania University of Brasov, Romania, that has formed me as an engineer and informaticien and has supported me to present and publish results of my research, including article *The Universal Law of Organization* - the scientific basis of this book.

To editors April Bogdon and Libbye Morris I say thank you for helping me to prepare the manuscript and for step-by-step careful, agreeable and generous leading along the self-publishing process of the first edition of this book with the title *„Critical Success Factors in Organization and Management."*

I would like to express my very great appreciation to entire team of CreateSpace Amazon Company for very well organized and managed self-publishing process and assistance, fact that minimizes the effort of authors and ensures the quality of books.

Many thanks to Assoc. Prof. Ph. D. Marin Vlada, University of Bucharest, Department of Applied Mathematics and Computer Science, who invited me to join a work at UB CNIV 2014, invitation as a result of which I have written this book.

My warmest thanks to eminent cardiologists and academics Dr. Ortan Ovidiu Florin - Head of Cardiology Emergency Section of Clinical County Hospital Brasov, and assistant professors at the Transilvania University of Brasov Dr. Rus Horatiu and Dr. Macasoi Petrisor Tudorel, without whose high quality intervention that saved my life, this book would not have been published.

Constantin Mihăescu

Introduction

"The role of a manual of chess is to teach you to think independently, so that you can win in all situations" **Dr. Max Euwe**

This manual of chess, business intelligence, and scientific management is addressed to students in the last years of high schools and universities, to managers of a small or medium business and generally to all those who wish to optimize their decisions.

It reveals three of the keys to success in business: 1) The scientific systemic vision of all things, phenomena and concepts, 2) The entirely new definition for scientific management based on *Universal Model of Organization and Management* - a true systemic management guide to maximize profits, and 3) Continuous business intelligence and management training.

The course is a natural reaction to the increasing complexity of problems in economy, which generates the corresponding need to increase the efficiency of solving methods that unfortunately have revealed their limits in the recent world economic crisis.

The scientific approach to concepts is vital for a more efficient organization and management of existing small and medium businesses, for creating of new profitable businesses and generally for problem-solving in complex real life situations.

The first researches for a scientific management were performed in the early twentieth century by the American engineer Frederick Winslow Taylor.

He first supported the need to establish ***"…a set of rules, laws and formulas to replace the judgment of each individual, but which can be used effectively only after they have been officially recorded." "…the best management is a true science, resting upon clearly defined laws, rules, and principles, as a foundation."***[1]

Shortly thereafter, the French engineer Henri Fayol

has identified five general management functions: planning, organizing, command, coordination and control.[2]

In order to support and complement these ideas, I offer in this book my latest research findings.

Albert Einstein wrote: ***"Scientific research is based on the idea that everything is determined by laws of nature, and therefore this holds for the actions of people."***

This idea has aroused my curiosity and desire to try to find out if for organization and management activities there is also a law of nature that governs them without us realizing it, as happened with the other laws of nature until they were discovered.

Without ever be explicitly referred to it, is easy to assume that Einstein inferred the existence of such a law.

Here's what he wrote in 1905, 50 years before he died: "I ***want to know how God created this world. I am not interested in this or that phenomenon, in the spectrum of this or that element. I want to know His thoughts; the rest are details."***

And later stated: ***"As a scientist, I believe that the***

nature is a perfect structure, looking through the perspective of reason and logic analysis."

Life is a continuous struggle to survive and to accomplish our goals and dreams, and all our activities are governed by natural laws.

Unfortunately, as a rule, in this struggle we do not use all of our mental resources, or we use them improperly, at random, without method.

Often this is a cause of our defeats, of our losses.

We can improve our thinking using a law of nature I recently discovered called "*The Universal Law of Organization*" and its logical graphic model, "*The Universal Model of Organization and Management*"[3] - both of which I present and use in this book.

According to my studies and numerous practical experiences, there is a law of nature that governs the organization and behavior of all self-organizing adaptive systems.

Using this law, its systemic vision, I have redefined the concepts of *organization, management* and *management functions* and this book will teach you how you can apply them easily to improve your decision support and business intelligence systems to maximize profit and your thinking to win in chess game and generally to be successful in life.

This model reveals the natural connections among all of these concepts, including how they are integrated in a perfectly self-organizing, adaptive system.

It will help you to improve the efficiency and effectiveness of any activity, including your business organization and management or your chess rating.

Thanks to this powerful natural model you will can better understand and better use the managerial concepts, in ways you never have before.

Now, for each one of managerial concepts you can find out different empirical definitions.

Although these definitions have proven their theoretical and practical utility, in literature on the subject emphasizes the need to solve the problem of this semantic variability, which negatively affects people's understanding of the concepts.

I hope that the new ideas in this book will help researchers in comparative international management field who want to discover managerial techniques that have universal validity.[4]

In many aspects, the world has a perfect logical structure and is governed by invariable and imperturbable laws of nature that can be discovered.

From microcosm to macrocosm, the world is organized into hierarchical levels, with systems coexisting harmoniously in a way that integrates subsystems from inferior levels into systems from superior levels.

Even the fundamental concepts of theoretical physics such as space, time, matter, energy and information are substantially tied to each other in such a way that the absence of one of them affects the very existence of the others.

In this perfectly organized world, each its component element or phenomenon can have only one single purpose, which is determined precisely by laws of nature based on its relationships with other elements and phenomena.

That is why each part or aspect of reality must be represented by a single unambiguous, scientific concept.

Therefore I hope that managers will agree with the concepts I have redefined on a scientific basis in this book and use them to increase their chances of success in business and in life.

Fundamental concepts of organization and management are here presented in systemic vision and then applied in chess to be fully clarified and thoroughly fixed in memory.

In this way, readers learn how to play well chess against the computer and also develop their self-control, self-confidence, critical and creative thinking, logic, memory and especially *imagination*.

In chess game, from beginning to the end, the player focuses on maximum to imagine and quickly implement strategic, tactical or logistical plans and decisions to solve problems that arise continually, one after another or simultaneously by every move of the opponent and that endanger victory.

And the development of imagination is more important than the accumulation of rational knowledge. A. Einstein wrote:

"Imagination is everything. Imagination is more important than knowledge. For knowledge is limited to all we now know and understand, while imagination embraces the entire world, and all there ever will be to know and understand." "The true sign of intelligence is not knowledge but imagination."

And about the game Einstein said: *"Play is the highest form of research."*

In general, given the universal model of organization and management, definition of *intelligence* could be this:

"The capacity to correctly and in-depth understand reality through processing gained knowledge and own observations and experiments, to discover new aspects of reality and to imagine new adaptive systems more efficient in order to solve problems, achieve goals or survival in difficult situations."

Therefore, imagination is an essential manifestation of intelligence, needed both in understanding reality and in solving problems.

In particular, according to Wikipedia, currently a widespread definition of *business intelligence* was formulated by Howard Dresner: *"Concepts and methods to improve business decision making by using fact-based support systems."*

Chess is rightly considered the king of games, the mind game, just given that it develops more than any other game human intelligence, imagination and many other capacities, qualities and skills.

Numerous studies and research have confirmed this extraordinary capacity of chess game, some of which can be found on the internet looking for example *"chess in schools"*.

In U.S., one of the first over 30 countries in the world which have introduced chess in schools, Chess Federation offers at a low price many such studies and research from entire world.

This book is the first scientific chess manual designed to teach basic knowledge of organization and management in systemic vision in schools, universities and all other educational institutions.

As manual, it can be used in at least three ways: 1) Classroom based training; 2) Web (computer) based training and 3) Self-study training.

Self-study training can be done anywhere, because the book is in pocket format and can thus accompany you everywhere.

You do not need chess pieces and chessboard, because presented games are set almost entirely in one diagram for each move, accompanied by comments on what happens in the game, mainly on each player's game plan and how he performs it.

From comments the reader understand how have been applied in game theoretical knowledge presented in the first two parts of the book, how the scientific method have been used, what does it mean thinking organized and managed in systemic vision.

Part one - THE BASIC CONCEPTS OF SCIENTIFIC MANAGEMENT

1. Why Do We Need Scientific Systems Approach for Concepts

Success depends on our ability to develop a feasible plan and then to execute it organizing and managing our actions using relevant concepts in a precise manner.

The fact that actual definitions of all managerial concepts differ according to their author, can be considered proof that they can be improved from the point of view of their precision.

The great scientist Albert Einstein said: **“I don’t like when it may be both in this way and in the other way. It should be this way, or not at all.”**

Empirical definitions are typically independent,

disconnected entities developed using the *analytic approach* which seeks to reduce a system to its elements and is less focused on interaction between them.

The *systemic approach* considers business organization and management as a complex, dynamic totality - as a system - and each component element as a part of this totality, strongly linked to the other parts by precise connections that have a great importance in obtaining profit maximization.

The System Concept

A system is an ensemble of elements functionally interrelated to achieve a common objective.

Few ideas can compete with the system concept in terms of importance.

During the last few decades, this concept generated a real revolution in science, accelerating the learning process in almost all fields.

This concept gives priority to the *whole* over the parts.

Where we see only disparate elements of a system, this concept attaches much importance to relationships and interactions among them, and it teaches us to understand the defined role of the individual elements as parts of the whole they compose.

Therefore this concept allows us to achieve a new mode of seeing and understanding things and phenomena.

It gives us a *systemic vision* on reality, a vision that is more profound and correct and that allows us to get better results in all fields of activity.

The Cybernetic Systems

Systems that have the ability to self-regulate are called ***cybernetic systems***.

The capacity of self-regulation of cybernetic systems is based on the so-called retroaction principle of *feedback*.

According to this principle, the system assigns values to the permanent results of an activity, compares them to the awaiting results (or objectives), and establishes deviations.

These deviations are transformed into actions that produce corrections in the system's work. Thanks to this mechanism of feedback, the system tends to eliminate its errors gradually, until the objectives are achieved.

Since 1948, *Cybernetics*, the science of feedback systems, has spread continuously and has received new definitions based on the fields to which researchers have applied it.

However, most of these definitions suggest the same idea: that ***cybernetics assures the best model for managing (regulating) complex processes, regardless of their nature***.

Organization of a Cybernetic System

Seen from outside, every cybernetic system is like a “black box", an opaque whole about which we know only that it hides an unknown process meant to achieve a certain purpose.

We can see only what gets in (input) and what gets out (output) from this box, not what happens inside.

If we open the box, we can observe the elements that compose the system, relationships among them, and the structure that allows one to achieve a defined goal (see Figure 1).

A system consists of at least two elements logically related to each other by their functions.

Taken separately, each element can be also considered a system.

Every system is formed by *subsystems* and can be considered at the same time a subsystem of a higher-leveled other system.

Therefore, there is a *hierarchy of systems* whereby the objectives of subsystems of a certain level derive from the objective of the system that these subsystems form, and so on.

If the system could be defined by its component elements statically, then dynamically it appears as a *typical complex of functional relations and interactions* among these elements.

These relations are not casual or changeable; they are derived precisely from the system's general objective.

That is why the system could be also defined as an *ensemble of tasks that are to be carried out under special conditions into a hostile environment.*

The *structure* of the system is defined by the construction, the architecture, and the way its parts are organized, closely depending on the whole they are forming.

The structure expresses quantitatively and qualitatively the content and internal constructive-functional logic.

The specific features of a system's structure derive from the interaction among components on the one hand, and between system's structure and its components, on the other hand.

Organization of not very complex systems needs

only three structural levels: a *system*, *subsystems* and *elements*.

The very complex systems have more hierarchical structural levels.

2. A Law of Nature: the Universal Model of Organization and Management. New Definitions of Concepts

Using the scientific method, I set out to develop new definitions of key concepts that correspond better to all characteristics of described entities, to real succession of their actions, and to connections among them or between them and their environment.

As I developed these new definitions, I ensured that they took into account *the space and time factors* and the basic principles of two sciences: *systemics* and *cybernetics.* That is how I formulated the model shown in Figure 1 and the proposed new definitions.

Later I observed that I cannot make any logical changes in this model but that it integrates logically all of other models and definitions under consideration.

This observation is one of the reasons I developed the "Universal Law of Organization[1]" which I defined as follows:

"The concepts concerning organizing activity are integrated naturally into a double feedback cybernetic system in conformity with a logical model called "The Universal Model of Organization and Management" (see Figure 1)

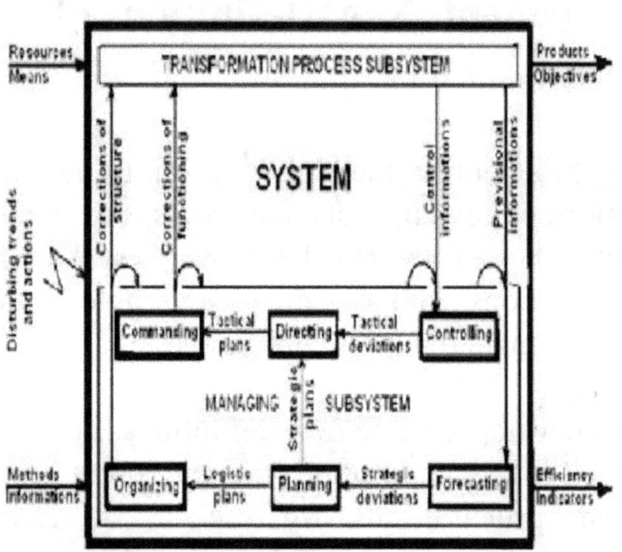

Figure 1: The Universal Model of Organization and Management

I integrated concepts into the model shown in Figure 1 using a strong logical requirement, as in the case of repairing a shattered vase from its pieces. Each concept had a unique right place, precisely determined by the necessity to fill it in a system as an indispensable natural component element.

The new definitions I am proposing, as they result from this logical model, are following:

- **The organizing activity** – Creates and improves system structure to be able to ensure achievement of certain objective in conditions of continuous fight against environment disturbing actions. Are projected and realized executive structure and management structure, all their component elements, connections between them or with environment. Also are elaborated their functioning rules.

- **The managing activity** – Orients, guides and regulates the system to work properly and efficiently to achieve the objective, without modifying its structure.

- The model I have proposed comprises two subsystems:

  - **The transformation process subsystem** which transforms physical resources in the product or result waited of system's work,

- **The managing subsystem which** collects information from both the system and the environment and makes rapid strategic, logistic and tactical decisions for elimination, decrease or compensation of disturbances occurred or anticipated in system's structure and functioning. This subsystem comprises two information management circuits:

    - The *tactical directing circuit* (into real time and on short-term time) which ensures the controlling function, directing function and commanding function.

    - The *strategic and logistic planning circuit* (in advance and on long-term time), which ensures the forecasting function, planning function and organizing function.

- **The three kinds of decisions:**

  - *Strategic decisions,* which order changes in strategy and make strategic plans.
  - *Logistic decisions,* which order changes in system's structure corresponding to changes in strategy and which make logistic plans.
  - *Tactical decisions,* which order corrections

in system functioning and make tactical plans.

- **The forecasting function** – Detects imminent disturbing tendencies and actions, evaluates their possible harmful influence on system's functioning, establishes that there are discrepancies between them and the current defense strategy, and identifies premises for their elimination, decrease, or compensation.
- **The planning function** – Allows the user to orient, plan and adjust strategic and logistic decisions in advance and, if necessary, adjust or change the objective. In addition, it follows, coordinates and ensures the completion of its decisions and plans.
- **The organizing function** – Elaborates procedures and projects that transform logistic decisions in corrections to system's structure, and ensures the availability of needed resources, and completion of these procedures and projects. If necessary, it creates or integrates subordinate subsystems into the system.
- **The controlling function** - Compares obtained results with expected results, and real functioning with normal functioning. Identifies tactical deviations and premises for their elimination, decrease, or compensation.
- **The directing function** - Makes tactical

decisions and defines tactical plans for elimination, decrease or compensation of deviations identified in system's functioning and for achievement of strategic plans.

- **The commanding function** – Provides commands to operate corrections to system functioning ordered by tactical decisions.

The management functions can be classified in three categories:

- *Analysis and synthesis functions* (forecasting and control)
- *Decision functions* (planning and directing)
- *Executing functions* (organizing and commanding

It is difficult to appreciate whether one of these functions is more important than other.

In case of systems created by men, the functions from strategic and logistic adjusting circuit have a great importance.

The analysis and synthesis functions, which must collect all necessary information for an efficient management, are often neglected. If this happens, it can hinder the system's ability to fulfill its objective and to survive.

3. Step-by-Step Guide of Scientific Business Organization and Management

I have shown that the ***system*** concept includes the interaction and correlation among component elements; in short, a system is an *organization as a whole.* From a systemic point of view, an *organization* is an *ensemble of actions that create or improve a systemic structure to achieve a certain goal.*

In nature, the most evolved systems are the biological systems. To survive, against disturbing environmental factors, they defend themselves by self-adapting (self-organizing) their structure and their behavior.

In business, if activities related to *organization* determine a business system's *statics* (structure), then activities related to *management* must determine the business system's *dynamics* (working and evolution).

Therefore, the manager can carry out his or her task in the best conditions only if the business process can be adjusted and adapted continuously, i.e. if it was previously organized as an *adaptive system.*

In this case, the system can be improved easily and continuously by using the *systemic approach* that incorporates the *Universal Model of Organization and Management* shown in Figure 1.This idea expresses the strong natural relationship between managing and organizing activities, which is the basis of *"Management in Systemic Vision"* or *"Scientific Management."*

Systemic Management

This method can be defined as *an integrated ensemble of ordered interdisciplinary principles, rules and actions by which a manager designs, plans, organizes his or her business as an adaptive whole (system), and guides (manages) it toward achievement of its objective.*

To plan (guide) a business system means to establish periodically which of the possible ways it has to act to attain its purpose on the condition of predictable and unpredictable oppositions.

In this case, the Universal Model of Organization and Management is used as a true *"business management compass."*

To direct (adjust) a business system means to act promptly to eliminate, minimize or compensate disturbances as soon as possible after they appeared in functioning.

In this case, the Universal Model of Organization and Management is used as an adjusting tool.

In adaptive cybernetic systems, both planning and adjusting actions are made by the *managing subsystem*.

The practical experience proves that to manage a

process efficiently, to ensure its steadiness and high-quality results, and to maximize profit, a manager must act using two information management circuits: the strategic (planning) circuit and tactical (directing) circuit.

Each of these two circuits has three management functions, as shown in Figure 1.

Discovered by observing and researching living systems, the method of *systemic management* can be now generalized in many fields, due to its simplicity, its accuracy and its high efficiency and effectiveness.

To organize a new business from scratch using this modern method, a managerial group can follow these eight steps:

1. Carefully and accurately set the desired outputs of your business system: the objective (product, service or solution to a problem), and efficiency indicators - taking into account current requirements, tendencies and risks in the market (See Figure 1).

2. Establish in detail the *transformation process*

subsystem (the business process) which transforms resources into the final product and takes into account efficiency indicators and available resources and means.

3. Determine the current and provisional information needed for control and forecasting functions of the managing subsystem and for the design of business information management software.

4. Establish the business strategic plan and its corresponding logistic plan, following current, short-term, medium-term and long-term business process adaptation to existing, imminent, or possible economic, social, and environmental changes.

5. Develop a program for organizing measures and allocating the resources needed for quick implementation of the business logistic plan.

6. Determine and engage the human resources that will be needed..

7. Train employees and test the business system functioning.

8. Start up the business system.

Initially, if company has a sole owner and fewer than five hundred employees, the managerial group can comprise only two members: the owner as general director and an accountant.

In some cases, depending on the company's size and complexity, the managerial team might need to be supplemented by a deputy director who provides supervision as well as accurate and just-in-time execution of decisions made by the general director.

Some of the most common reason that businesses fail are a lack of experience and limited management knowledge.

Before a manager attempts a business start-up, he or she must have enough knowledge of organization and management to ensure good results from the beginning.

Spending a couple of hours reading this book should provide enough knowledge for this purpose.

Part two -THINKING OPTIMIZATION PROCESS IN CHESS GAME

4. Optimization Process of Chess Players' Thinking by Scientific Organization and Management

Wanting to be as possible very suggestive and easy to understand for all readers was very difficult for me to choose improved activity to give you as example in this case study.

Finally, I decided to choose the subject of thinking in chess game, because, according to a Chinese proverb, *"Life is like a game of chess, changing with each move"*

Indeed, chess is no doubt the most analogous strategic board game ever invented to simulate military battles or, who knows, even the battles in the complex "game" of life.

Our lives (for the long term) and our activities (for

the short and medium term) are indeed like chess games. T. H. Huxley said: "Yet, it is a very plain and elementary truth that the life, the fortune, and the happiness of every one of us, and, more or less, of those who are connected with us, do depend upon our knowing something of the rules of a game infinitely more difficult and complicated than chess. It is a game that has been played for untold ages, every man and woman of us being one of the two players in a game of his or her own. The chess-board is the world, the pieces are the phenomena of the universe, and the rules of the game are what we call the laws of Nature."

There are so many similarities between life battles - including business - and chess, so scientists, even some Nobel Prize in Economic Sciences Laureates (H. Simon in 1978, J. F. Nash in 1994, and R. J. Aumann and T. C. Schelling in 2005), used it as tool for economic research and discoveries. All mental tools used to win in a chess game are useful for our success in business and in life.

The following examples are from chess game scientific thinking organization and management.

At first sight, the problem we intend to solve at the chess table could be formulated as follows: Starting from the initial position, how must we move our own pieces so that, at a given moment, our opponent could not avoid "mate"?

However, this first formulation is only apparently right. Usually, games between high performance chess players do not end in mate: one of them resigns when his or her opponent has a positional superiority enough to win. We call this moment of the game the “moment of effective superiority” (MES). Now, it seems that we can reformulate correctly the problem if we replace “*mate*” with “*effective superiority*”.

We would be wrong once again -- although less than in the first formulation -- because a careful analysis of great masters’ games reveals that, in fact, fight is decided even earlier, when one of the players has discovered a plan that is superior to that of his or her opponent. This is the *Moment of Potential Superiority* (MPS). In a precise game, what follows this moment is only a technical demonstration done by the owner of the better plan in the effort to accomplish it and to obtain the MES.

But what is *a good plan*? We evaluate the plan after its results. A good plan is that which, in spite of adversary’s opposition and using all resources at best, gets to purpose: breaking initial balance of forces, obtaining a material or/and positional superiority enough to win. A special category of good plans is those that create a very complex position and opponent falls in time crisis.

To impose his aggressive plan and to combat adverse opposition, each player takes decisions that are carried out in moves. If these moves are well planned and produce counted effects, they can be considered *active moves*. Therefore, we call "*active move*" a move that weakens the opponent's position and/or prepares application of a successful "knock out".

Moves can be:

- Purely offensive;
- Offensive defensive;
- Defensive offensive;
- Purely defensive.

The moves purely offensive, offensive defensive and defensive offensive are active moves.

The purely defensive moves, if they are not forced, as well as those that are only apparently active (which follow a plan that proves to be wrong. i.e. can be integrated in the adversary's plan) are considered *inactive moves.*

The more active moves are achieved from the total of all played moves, the more powerful and productive a player's thinking is.

It results that a good plan, composed of active moves, is truly anticipated product of a chess player's thinking system. Wrong plans and moves are rejected and therefore cannot count in the productivity calculation of a chess player's thinking system.

The most important objective in a chess game is to obtain first a good plan and to accomplish it making only active moves to achieve quickly a superiority enough to obtain victory. The rest of game is routine.

In chess, there are two kinds of resources: 1) T*echnical resources:* game preparation time, game thinking time, tempo reserve (for example first 40 moves in 2 hours), space (a part of the 64 squares on the chess board) and material (16 pieces), and *2) Information or intellectual resources:* information, methods, psychological processes, thinking ability, general and special preparation etc..

Grandmasters have often succeeded in games in which each tempo used becomes an active move. A scientific method must help the chess player elaborate and apply an efficient plan quickly and accurately so that he or she can reach MES before the adversary does.

Elaboration and implementation a plan are operations that are characteristic of the activity of management. If a chess player wants to succeed, this activity should develop in accordance with the organizing and managing model shown in Figure 1.

You can achieve an efficient chess game's management only if you organize both the managed process and thinking management activities using the Universal Model of Organization and Management.

Starting from the necessity of victory and passing back through the chain of logical relations among the notions of victory, the moment of effective superiority, the moment of potential superiority, a good plan, - the chess player achieves a complete image of the route to victory and understands that on this logical route he or she must go with a specially adapted vehicle: a specialized scientific thinking system.

The scientific organization of the chess player's thinking system is an activity through which all information and notions that could help us win are identified, rigorously defined, classified and structured in our memory as a cybernetic thinking system using the Universal Model of Organization and Management. Developing such a system will help the player make the optimum play during every moment of chess game.

5. Organizational and Managerial Requirements in the Chess Players' Thinking That Will Help Them Use All Resources Efficiently

To help a player use all resources efficiently, I have formulated the following requirements:

A. Requirements for organizing game thinking time:

- Use both your own thinking time and your opponent's thinking time in a way that achieves maximum productivity at your play. Transfer some thinking operations performed during your time to your opponent's time.
- Organize your thinking time into three categories: time for active moves (time used productively), time not used, and time used inadequately.
- Maximize the amount of time you use for active moves.

B. Requirements for organizing game preparing time

- Spend most of your time in highly productive preparing activities.
- Consider this book a deposit of sufficient knowledge to assure players high performance without supplementary documentation.
- Use guidelines from this book to improve your methods of study, practice, and documentation, so that you waste a minimum of time due to imperfections.

C. Requirements for organizing the use of *tempo* (turns, moves) *reserve*:

- According to the player interest, there are only three categories of moves: proper active moves, inactive moves and adversary's active moves (disturbing for us).

- Then, the organization must:

- Take into account only the three categories of moves just mentioned.
- Specify the criteria according to which every move could be included precisely in one of these categories and the best tactics to follow in every case;
- Demonstrate how to increase number of

active moves despite other move categories.

D. Requirements for space utilization:

- Space is a resource with special features. Unlike the resources of time (thinking time, preparing time, tempos), whose consumption is definitive and irreversible, space is a resource that can be used repeatedly (discontinuously)..
- Your *reserve of space* includes all squares controlled by your pieces. A controlled square is that square where a piece is, where it can move, or where it only exerts its influence without the possibility of occupying it in the next move.
- To gain a superior position and more space, use organized thinking to find ways to increase controlled space and to decrease space that could be useful to your opponent.

E. Requirements for organizing of material utilization:

- Demonstrate the possibility that you can involve some of the opponent's pieces to reach your plan.
- Divide all pieces on the chess board into three categories used by you, used by your opponent, and unused.
- Use valid criteria to estimate the relative value of pieces according to which a piece can be

included in one of these categories and can be estimated in comparison to other pieces.

- Present the means by which you can improve the structure of pieces involved in the game by increasing the number of pieces that are useful to you.

.

F. Organization of information and intellectual resources.

It is difficult to know how the brain works. In this case, can we improve our thinking, - a mechanism about whose inner working we do not know enough?

This is not an impossible task: it is possible because activity that takes place in the most complex biological organ – the human brain - is endowed with a special property: *the capacity of self-instruction and self-improvement*.

Human brain, in its immense network of cells, contains a number of circuits. We obtain most of the logical connections among these cells – namely our knowledge and habits in our life - during the process of conscious learning (self-instruction) or unconscious learning (experience).

Without knowing enough about thinking, we cannot improve it directly, but we can indirectly. One of these ways consists of grafting in our mind of an efficient scientific *thinking model* able to answer successfully to all above demands of organization, to solve all special problems that can appear during game management.

Once learned, this model will replace the old inefficient, not specialized, and empirical thinking.

This idea leads to the formulation of a unique specialized scientific model for organizing and managing a chess player's thinking.

The player's training using this model ensure quick and correct decisions of moves to take in any moment of the game: thinking must proceed in such a way that permits the optimum use of all resources, stimulates his or her imagination, ensure a harmonious combination of logic and judgment, and allows direct or adapted use of typical solutions stored in memory.

This model reduces the player's need to make low speed calculations for validation of solutions. Mind resources are used as algorithms, as well as specific highly-organized proceedings so that the player can spend less thinking time but still make accurate decisions.

Finally, this new model of thinking optimizes the

player's use of memory and helps him or her avoid being distracted by knowledge that is not likely to be used.

6. The Model of Chess Game as a Cybernetic System

Considering the ideas revealed above, now we can build a model of a cybernetic system of thinking in the chess game.

Apart from its basic structure shown in Figure 1, this model has a feature related strictly to specifics of a chess game: the functions of organizing and *commanding* are unified into a single modulus.

This is because the succession of moves forming *the program* (a variant that will be played) can include alternatively or simultaneously strategic and tactical aspects in each move.

Each move can be both a strategic move and a tactical move simultaneously.

In this model, the managed process represents the totality of events occurring physically on the chess board.

The moves are made observing the whole set of rules written into regulations of the game or learned by the player during special study.

At each move we spend (use) *a thinking time*, *a piece* (giving it a role in the game plan; a piece usually is not available for other roles), *a tempo* (the right to move once), and *a square* (a physical space on which we move).

In exchange for these expenses, we gain *a new position* (the product of the chess game system).

This position can be good for us if our good plan has been executed correctly. But every time it follows an opponent's move that causes *disturbances* in our plan.

Evaluation of the achievement level of the plan, identification of disturbances caused by the opponent, and estimation of situation are all achieved by means of specific information that allows us to "read" essential aspects in our position.

In the chess game system, *"the process"* is the chain of our transforming operations of game resources, and of the opponent's disturbing actions in successive positions

The resulting positions are characterized by the place occupied by each piece on the chess board (concrete aspect) and by relations among pieces according to the rules of the game (abstract aspects).

The "*managed process*" is the succession of positions, the evolution of relations (simple or complex) among pieces, events that take place on chess board, and the entire multitude of specific relations and events (usually unperceived or partially perceived by us now), no matter how many there are and how complicated they should.

A chess player become more skilled as he or she is able to perceive more aspects of this multitude, and to classify them more rapidly and correctly into essential and non-essential in every moment of the game.

The "*managing process*" (i.e. the player's thinking) takes place in player's mind, *over* the chess board, not *on* it, as in the case of the managed process.

This process *plans* the achievement of our potential superiority and *directs* the transformation of the chess resources in terms of the various positions.

"*Planning*" a managed process, means to establish a way by which a player can achieve positional superiority despite his or her opponent's resistance.

"*Directing*" a managed process means a player makes moves to accomplish plan and to eliminate, decrease, or compensate as soon as possible any disturbances caused by opponent's moves.

The managing subsystem (process) can be divided into six elements or *component modules,* as follows:

On the *directing circuit* are these modules: tactical analysis of position, elaboration of short-term-plans (*tactical plans*), and *applying program* for these tactical plans.

On *the planning circuit* are these modules: strategic analysis of position, elaboration of long-term-plans *(strategic plans)* and *applying program* for these strategic plans.

The applying modules of the strategic plans and the tactical plans have been unified into a single one: *the modulus of elaboration and implementation of the program* (the succession of selected moves to be played).

Within the *strategic analysis of position,* using *the module of strategic analysis,* a chess player collects strategic information, analyzes them, tries to anticipate tendencies in the game's development, and evaluate their negative consequences.

At the same time establishes eventual disaccords (*strategic deviations*) between his or her own current strategic plan and the correct winning strategic plan, and if the opponent can exploit them.

Similarly, *tactical analysis of position* finds *tactical deviations* as well as the premises of exploiting of these deviations by the opponent..

To *elaborate the strategic plan,* a player exploits strategic weaknesses of his or her opponent's position or plan, and the defense premises of his or her own weaknesses in position.

In addition, the player chooses the most convenient aspects that can be unified in a strategic plan in a couple of moves.

This player's strategic plan combines important decisions that establish evolution and adaptation of own game to the anticipated changes in position.

Strategy is defined as a way to be followed so that one can achieve an objective.

Strategic decisions guide the orientation of the game on long term, global modalities associated with transforming position resources, taking the opponent's actions and resistance into account.

Elaboration of the tactical plan carries out the adjusting function to implement the strategic plan, eliminate or compensate disturbances caused by adversary's moves and achieve one's objective in spite of them.

Based on the premises found by analysis, the player establishes in detail the most convenient practical modalities for achieving strategy and exploiting weaknesses and errors in opponent's game, and for a rapid and efficient mobilization of necessary resources and means for attack and for defense stratagems.

While *strategy* establishes the direction, the orientation of player's actions, *what* must be done to acquire potential superiority, t*actics* establishes *with what* pieces, *where, when* and *how* the player will operate to achieve the strategic plan.

Tactical decisions are prompt "reactions" to the opponent's moves and cause actions that have a double purpose, for example to fight against the disturbing influences of an opponent's move and simultaneously to achieve a component of implementing program of one's strategic plan.

Compared to strategy, which typically requires many moves, tactics needs only one or a few moves, preferably forced.

While strategy organizes changes in the structure of a fight device, in location and collaboration between pieces, tactics allows quick decisive strokes.

If tactical blows are not decisive, they should be applied only if not harm the strategic plan adopted by the player.

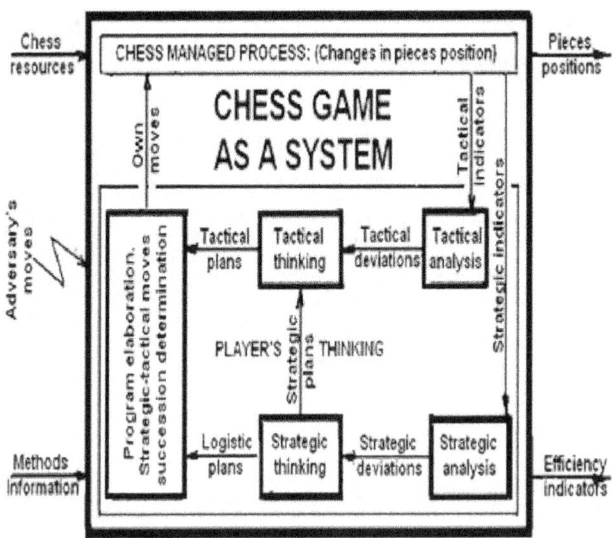

Figure 2: The model of chess game as a system

The *program of moves* results from fusion of a strategic-logistic plan with a tactical plan and some intermediary moves (necessary to execute an immediate defense or a quick tactical stroke) in each move (See Figure 2) This fusion allows optimization of a succession of moves and consumption of fewer resources for maximum rapidity and efficiency in achieving the objective.

Once a chess player's thinking is organized using the model in Figure 2, he or she begins the final stage of self-improvement: testing this new thinking system in practical chess games.

It is obvious that we can never get to manage the

chess game process efficiently before knowing its complex details.

The detailed and complete analysis of the chess game as a system supposes to analyze, in systemic vision, every detail of the model shown in Figure 2.

Only in this way will we discover all of the secrets of this miraculous game and all the winning practical rules that results by analogy for organization and management of all our activities in business or life.

But such a detailed and complete analysis exceeds the limits of this book. I set out to show, in generally, how you can apply the Universal Model of Organization and Management to any activity in an effort to increase its efficiency and effectiveness and achieve success.

For mangers who want to self-improve their thinking by analyzing or playing chess, and for advanced chess players, I written a book entitled *Chess and Cybernetics*[5] into which I made such a scientific, detailed and complete analysis of winning player's thinking in a chess game as a system.

In business, as in life, the success depends mainly on the quality and force of your most important resource: *thinking,* on its level of scientific organization and management.

Reading *Chess and Cybernetics*, more than in this book, you are learning how to use methodically and efficiently your thinking and other main resources: time, space, energy, materials and information.

It can help you to self-organize and manage your thinking so that you can achieve a high level of performance in all your activities, including business.

Why chess? Because the chess game perfectly simulates life, the hard struggle for survival and achievement of our objectives.

Reading this new book, you will enjoy like never before the most hidden, fascinating secrets of chess combat.

And, by analogy, you will draw theoretical and practical conclusions about ways for improve your business and your life.

Why cybernetics? Because to survive and to succeed in business or life, you must always react as cybernetic systems: acting quickly and correctly against current or anticipated disturbing factors of environment, and self-organizing and managing all of your activities with a scientific method.

Chess and Cybernetics contains about 300 pages and 250 chess diagrams from thematic commented games of some of most powerful grandmasters and chess world champions.

It is a manual about *scientific chess* and, by analogy, about *fight science*, *business science,* and life science.

Part three – THE SCIENTIFIC STUDY OF CHESS GAMES AGAINST COMPUTER

7. Chess Games Won by Former World Champion Garry Kasparov against IBM's Deep Blue Supercomputer. The Continuous Active Limitation of Opponent's Game Opportunities

7.1. The Sixth Game of the Match, Philadelphia, 02.16.1996 Opening: Queen's Gambit Declined

White: Garry Kasparov Black: Deep Blue. Source: http://ro.wikipedia.org/wiki/Deep_Blue#cite_note-as-20

1.Nf3 d5 2. d4 c6 3. c4 e6 4. Nbd2 Nf6 5. e3 c5 6. b3 Nc6 7. Bb2 cxd4 8. exd4 Be7 9. Rc1 O-O 10. Bd3 Bd7 11. O-O Nh5 12. Re1 Nf4 13. Bb1 Bd6 14. g3 Ng6 15. Ne5 Rc8 16. Nxd7 Qxd7 17. Nf3 Bb4 18. Re3 Rfd8 19. h4 Nge7 20. a3 Ba5 21. b4 Bc7 22. c5 Re8 23. Qd3 g6 24. Re2 Nf5 25. Bc3 h5 26. b5 Nce7 27. Bd2 Kg7 28. a4 Ra8 29.a5 a6 30. b6 Bb8 31. Bc2 Nc6 32. Ba4 Re7 33. Bc3 Ne5 34. dxe5 Qxa4 35. Nd4 Nxd4 36. Qxd4 Qd7 37. Bd2 Re8 38. Bg5 Rc8 39. Bf6+ Kh7 40. c6 bxc6 41. Qc5 Kh6 42. Rb2 Qb7 43. Rb4 1-0

Skillfully combining in every move defense with aggressive intentions, tactical solutions with respect to the strategic plan pursued from start to finish, Kasparov managed to get step by step small positional advantages of development and space, which gradually have amounted to almost complete blocking of black pieces.

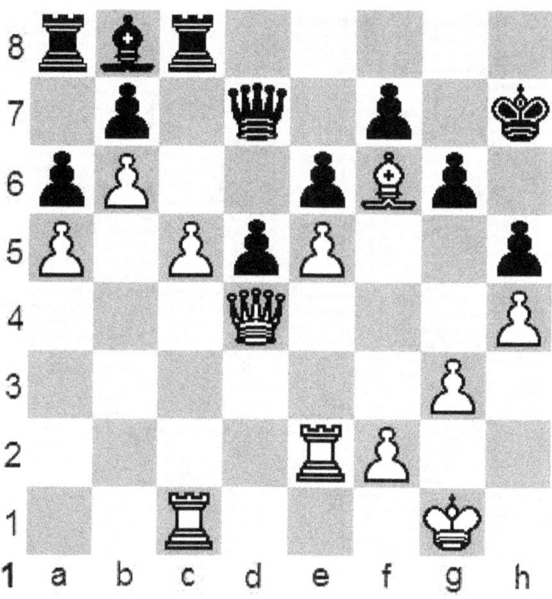

Position after move 39...Kh7

This position was reached after White avoided permanently the opening of the game, thus limiting the extraordinary opponent's ability to perform tactical combinations in open positions. As shown, after 39 moves each player still has seven pawns on the board!

Followed 40.c6!!... a strategic pawn sacrifice which has created a white passed pawn on b6, well defended and supported, threatening to turn into queen in just two moves.

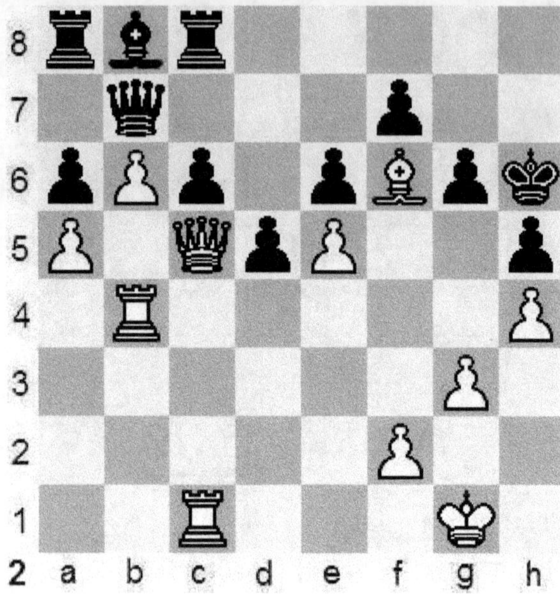

Position after move 43. Rb4!

This is the final position appearing after only four moves to position on previous diagram.

Black gave up because it is almost completely blocked and cannot simultaneously prevent the threat of conversion of free white advanced pawn b6 to queen and black protector pawn chain breakage threat of move g3-g4 followed by quick-destroying attack with all white figures on defenseless black king.

An excellent demonstration of permanent active limitation of opponent's attack ability using always moves with a quadruple character: defender-attacker and strategic-tactical.

7.2. The First Game of the Match, New York 05.03.1997 Opening: King's Indian Defense.

White: Garry Kasparov Black: Deep Blue. Source: http://ro.wikipedia.org/wiki/Deep_Blue#cite_note-as-20

1. Nf3 d5 2. g3 Bg4 3. b3 Nd7 4. Bb2 e6 5. Bg2 Ngf6 6. O-O c6 7. d3 Bd6 8. Nbd2 O-O 9. h3 Bh5 10. e3 h6 11. Qe1 Qa5 12. a3 Bc7 13. Nh4 g5 14. Nhf3 e5 15. e4 Rfe8 16. Nh2 Qb6 17. Qc1 a5 18. Re1 Bd6 19. Ndf1 dxe4 20. dxe4 Bc5 21.Ne3 Rad8 22. Nhf1 g4 23. hxg4 Nxg4 24. f3 Nxe3 25. Nxe3 Be7 26. Kh1 Bg5 27. Re2 a4 28. b4 f5 29. exf5 e4 30. f4! Bxe2 31. fxg5 Ne5 32. g6! Bf3 33. Bc3 Qb5 34. Qf1 Qxf1+ 35. Rxf1 h5 36. Kg1 Kf8 37. Bh3! b5 38. Kf2 Kg7 39. g4! Kh6 40. Rg1 hxg4 41. Bxg4 Bxg4 42.Nxg4+ Nxg4+ 43. Rxg4 Rd5 44. f6 Rd1 45. g7 1-0

To avoid opening of the game early, White has chosen a less studied and played opening and delayed as he could to occupy the center with its pawns and pieces.

It was not until the 15th move that White has placed a pawn well defended in center, on the fourth line, still keeping all other pieces on the first three lines, with pawns in front.

Advancing its pawns, Black tried unsuccessfully to break White's position and to create weaknesses that then attack them. White's position remained solid, without weaknesses, with pieces in perfect collaboration and ready to launch an attack on the kingside.

In Black's position appeared strategic weaknesses difficult to identify by computer that Kasparov had exploited promptly and skillfully.

White has found a strategic-tactical maneuver that created two connected passed white pawns well supported on the kingside.

Being less skilled in strategy than in tactics, Black underestimated great danger generated by these two pawns (see below position after moves: 28 (diag. 1), 29 (diag. 2), 30 (diag. 3), 31(diag. 4) and 32 (diag. 5). Seeing that these two white pawns cannot be stopped to advance and be promoted, Black resigns at move 45 (see diag. 6).

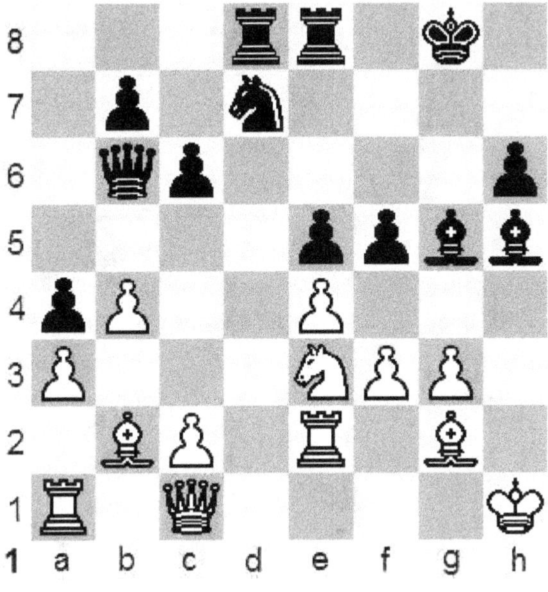
1

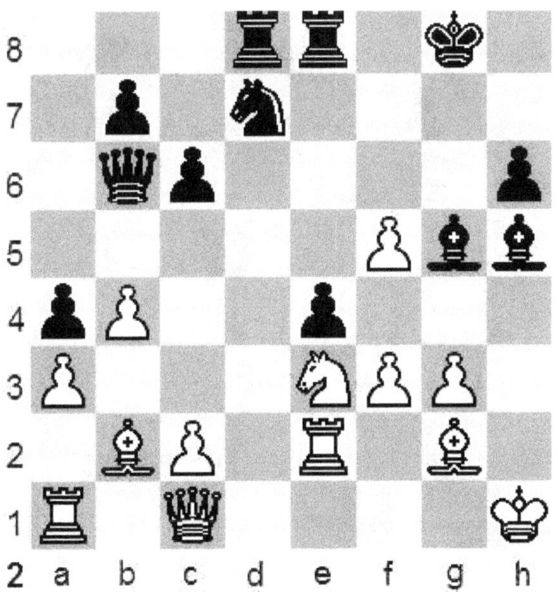
2

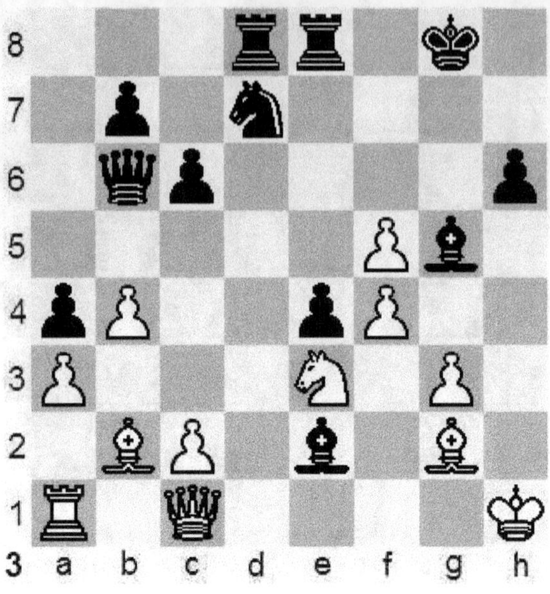
3

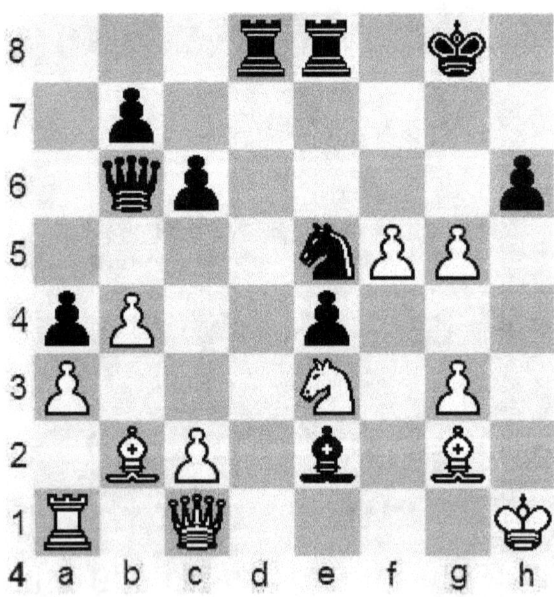
4

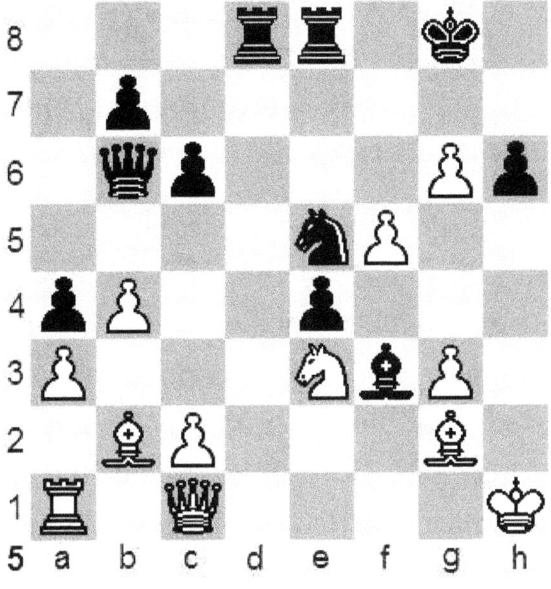

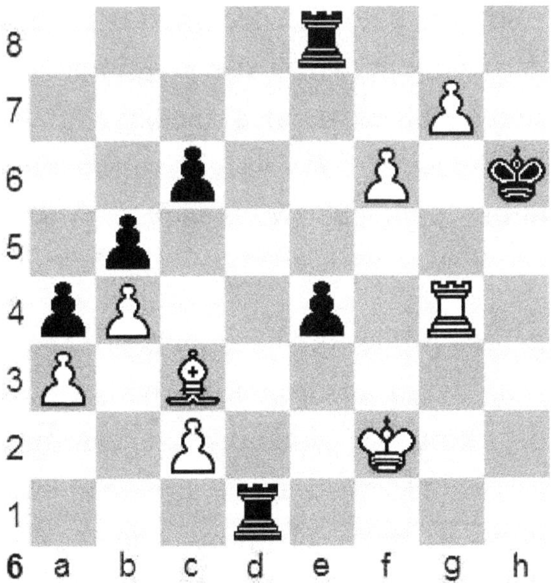

7.3. Continuous Active Limitation of Opponent's Game Opportunities

Careful study of these two games above (of one who for 15 years has held the title of world champion) as can be clearly reveals that one of the most effective methods to combat chess computer is keeping the game closed, limiting opportunities of adverse pieces to advance on active positions in and to our position and postponing major tactical confrontations as many moves as possible until preparations of our attack will be completed.

Doing so, we gain the necessary time to imagine and get move by move small positional advantages which summed allow us at a special moment (that I called "the *Moment of Potential Superiority* " - MPS) the beginning of a decisive attack against opposing king.

This active limitation of opponent's game is the only way to avoid confrontation with entire terrible and rapid computing capacity of chess machine, its spectacular and often unpredictable tactical combinations in open positions and to force it to accept confrontation between the strategic ideas in which it does not excel.

Human imagination in terms of developing strategies has no limits and is more productive and spectacular as it operates in more complicated positions with several pieces and along several moves.

To illustrate the exceptional importance of strategy of active limitation of opponent's game even in the simplest positions, I chose the following study by Maizelis (1921). White to move wins unless by active moves limiting Black's game (see diag. 1):

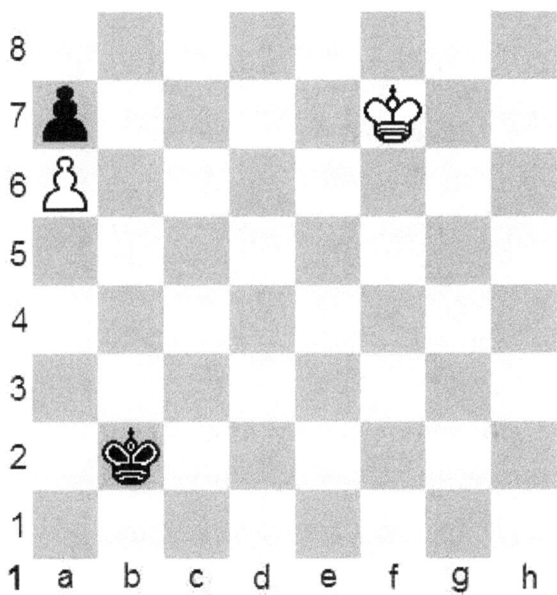

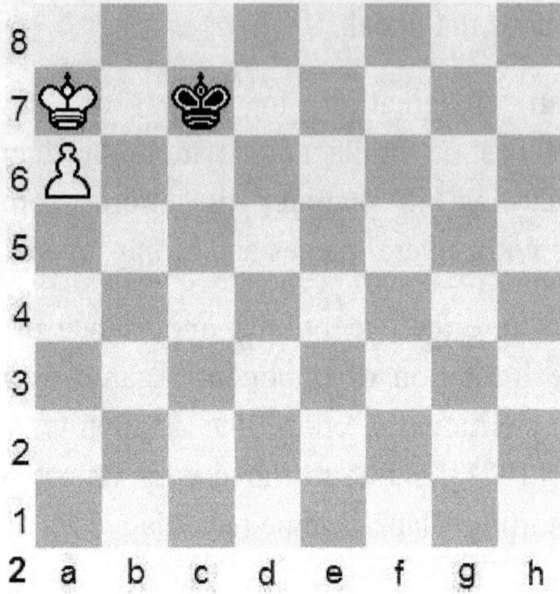

Position analysis shows that White wins only if, after taking the black pawn, can leave the fields in front of his own pawn.

To do this, he must not allow Black to reach the position in diag. 2 and get a draw.

In his way to black pawn a7, White must play so that in each move he combines the limitation of Black's possibilities to get closer to square c7 with getting closer to black pawn to capture it when Black cannot occupy the field c7 next move.

In other words, the limitation of opponent's game must be active, i.e. to add with each move another contribution to the achievement of the strategic or tactical plan. In each move the **defensive** and opponent's game **limiting** character must be combined with the **active aggressive** character of own game (see Ch. 4 – *active move*).

Specifically, in this study, if White plays hurry apparently correct move 1. Ke7? he misses victory as follows 1 ... Kc3 2. Kd7 Kd4 3. Kc7 Kd5 4. Kb7 Kd6 5. Kxa7 Kc7 draw.

Move 1. Ke7? is wrong because only meet active aggressive character and ignore the defensive limiting of Black's possibilities of reaching square c7.

To fulfill the defensive limiting of opponent's game character, on its way to capturing black pawn a7, White should come out to meet the black king to limit its mobility, so as to prevent it in time to reach savior square c7.

White's gain maneuver is simple and very instructive, which is why remember it in your game can be very useful.

In the first two moves white king is moving toward two targets simultaneously: the opposing pawn and the "gate" composed of squares c4 and d4 the black king must pass in its second move in the way to c7.

Occupying at the second move d5 square, White places in front of black king timely an impassable "barrier" which makes it to lose a precious tempo and with it the game.

So White will have to continue like this:**1. Ke6! Kc3 2. Kd5! Kb4 3. Kc6 Ka5 4. Kb7 Rb5** (Black king is forced to remain a tempo on the fifth rank, having no accessible way to go near c7-square) **5. Kxa7 Kc6 6. Kb8** and White wins.

During the whole game, we must strive to get active limiting of adverse pieces' mobility and aggressiveness, by preventing them from occupying or controlling squares close or into our position, dislocating and maintaining them in marginal positions or in which they lock each other, crowding them.

This strategy must be applied simultaneously with active maneuvers to obtain positional advantages, as brilliantly showed us Garry Kasparov in the above two games, won against the strongest chess computer in the world.

8. Games Won by Author against Winboard 2.0 GNU Chess Engine Using Scientific Management

In the following games, each pair of moves is shown in a chess diagram accompanied by a comment which explains the main intentions and achievements of players, the manner in which each organizes his position, strategic or tactical plan followed, how they manage their resources, briefly the organization and management of their thinking according to new concepts and rules of systemic organization and scientific management shown in previous chapters.

This mode of presentation in a continuous sequence of images (diagrams) greatly facilitates the understanding of players' thinking along the entire game, because it is known that *a picture is worth a thousand words* and that in teaching process filmed lessons are sometimes preferable, being most effective.

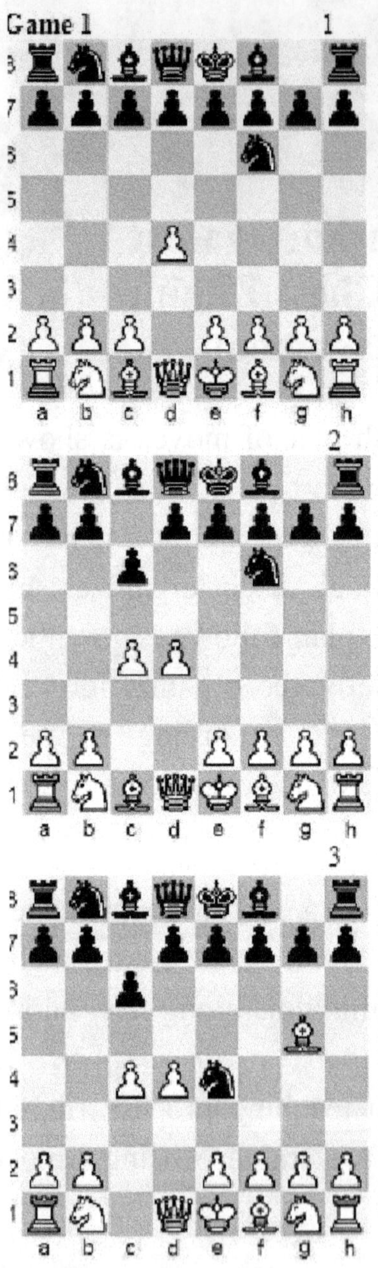

White: C. M. Black: Computer

1. d2-d4 Ng8-f6

To avoid tactical complications in which Black is big expert, White's strategic plan aims from the beginning to close the game on q-side, delay the activation of black pieces, decrease of their space for maneuver, agglomerate them on k-side and then give by surprise the final attack on other side using the strongest piece: the queen.

2. c2-c4 c7-c6

White allows his queen go to b3 or c2 and fast entering into play of neighboring pieces in order to perform queenside castling. Black begins to anticipate and memorize weaknesses in White's position and prepares to attack them immediately. With the move c7-c6, Black plans to attack the pawn on b2 with its queen on b6 and thus to take the initiative.

3. Bc1-g5 Nf6-e4

White wants elimination of black f6-knight because in expected closed positions knights are more valuable than bishops. If Black plays 3 .. h6 to dislocate bishop from g5, then White plays 4.Bxf6 and after 4...exf value of f7- and f6- black pawns decreases. Black's knight leaves the attacked f6-square and in turn attacks the defenseless g5-bishop.

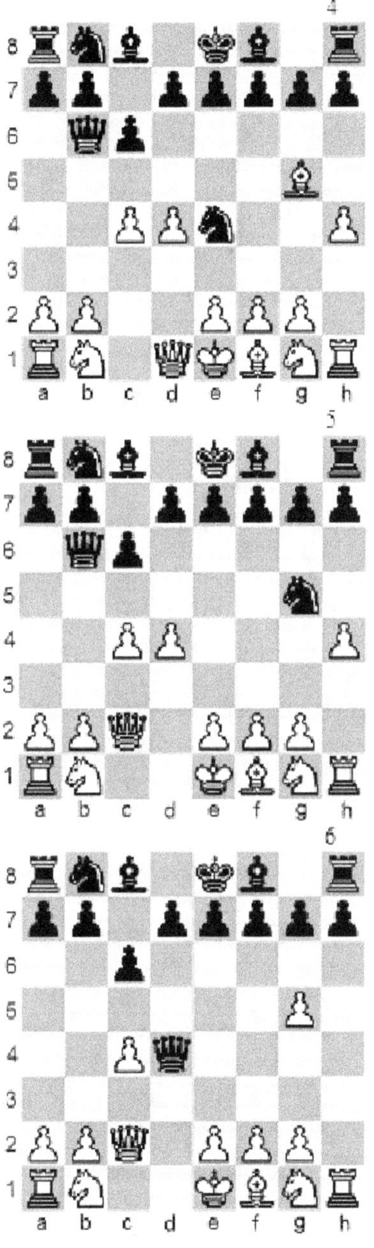

4. h2-h4 Qd8-b6

White chooses the most active continuation: defends the bishop on g5 with a move that brings two more pieces in play: the h-pawn and the h-rook. This defense does not delay his strategic plan, but rather increases the pressure on the k-side. Black does not miss the opportunity to attack the pawn on b2 immediately.

5. Qd1-c2! Ne4xg5

White defends the pawn on b2 and offers the sacrifice of d4-pawn in order to get then an important advantage in development of his pieces. The move 5. b2-b3 would have weakened the a2-b2-shield of pawns which must be kept to protect the white king after the queenside castling. And the withdrawal of g5-bishop would have meant an unacceptable double waste of tempo.

6. h4xg5 Qb6xd4

Black does not see the White's strategic trap. In its calculations on several moves ahead, Black finds no material losses, accepts the sacrifice proposed by its opponent and captures the d4-pawn. But this hasty capture and the exchange of the minor pieces on g5 caused it an extremely important triple loss of tempo which will decide the fate of the game in favor of White.

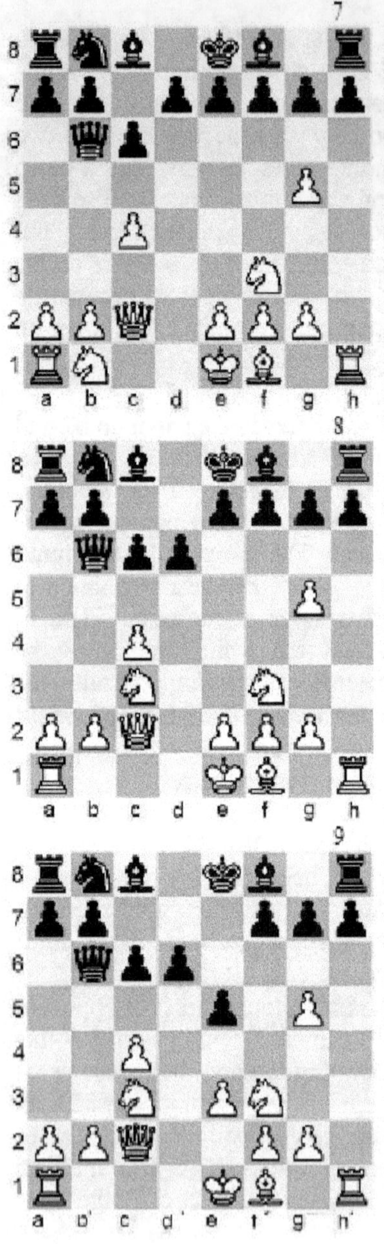

7. Ng1-f3 Qd4-b6
White brings another minor piece into play. Black cannot do the same; it is obliged to withdraw the queen and because of this it loses another tempo in development of its pieces. It has only two active pieces, while White has five! To make castling, White has to move twice, while Black has to move four times, because previously it must defend the h7-pawn attacked by two white major pieces.

8. Nb1-c3 d7-d6
White prepares q-side castling and also brings into play another minor piece in a square from where next move it can attack the black queen, forcing it to retreat and lose a tempo again. The Black's move aims to clear the way for c8-bishop to go into battle, and also to support desired advancement of e7-pawn to e5.

9. e2-e3 e7-e5
White postpones castling in order to can move 10. Be2 after Black's move 9...Bg4, and thus to offer a exchange of minor pieces on f3 for him only favorable, because it brings into play the white bishop on f3, while c8-bishop disappears together with two tempos spent on its moves. Black prepares 10...Be7 to attack on g5.

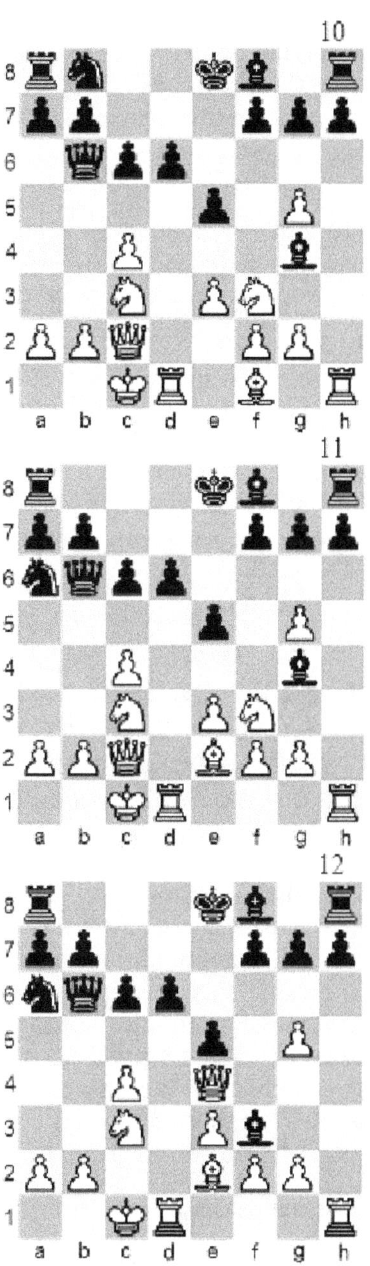

10. 0-0-0 Bc8-g4

With this fast queenside castling, preparations of White's kingside attack are almost finished and his positional superiority is evident. Further White will try to transform this superiority into victory using moves that combine complex strategic maneuvers with tactical unexpected attacking combinations and strikes. Bishop on g4 binds White's Knight on f3.

11. Bf1-e2 Nb8-a6

White unbinds immediately his f3 knight and brings into battle a new minor piece: the bishop on e2. In this moment all White's pieces are in active positions and having much excellent opportunities to collaborate into kingside attack. Black prepares queenside castling and the attack with its knight from b4 to the White's c2-queen and a2-pawn.

12. Qc2-e4! Bg4xf3

With this unexpected second move in opening of his queen, White threatens to capture the bishop on g4 and brings his strongest piece in center to increase pressure on Black's defensive device. Black accepts the exchange of minor pieces and hopes that White's response will be 13. Be2xf3 that then allows it to make queenside castling next move.

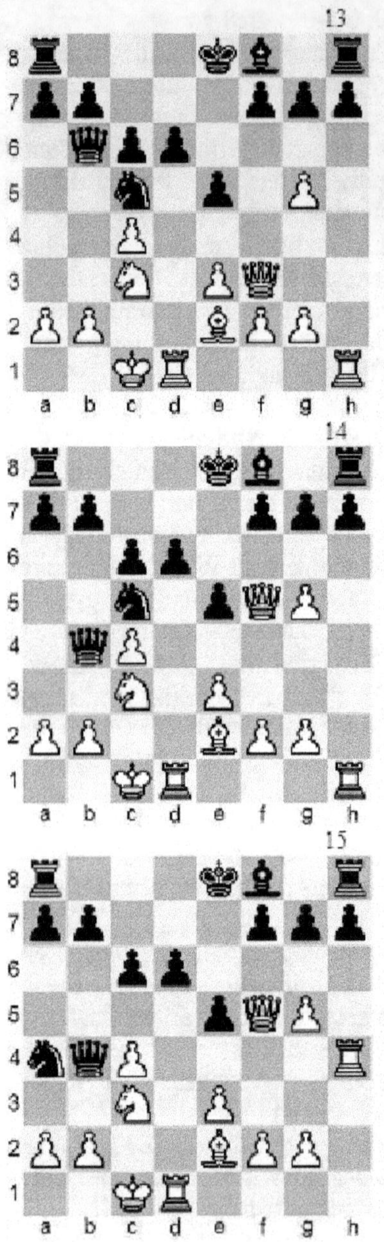

13. Qe4xf3! Na6-c5

White chooses a less expected move, but which serves perfectly achieving of his strategic plan. On f3 queen threatens the f7-pawn which can be captured if Black makes queenside castling. Because of this, black king is forced to remain in center, where it is more vulnerable to White's treats. White has a great positional advantage.

14. Qf3-f5! Qb6-b4

White makes a new strategic move designed to take under control the h3-c8 diagonal and thereby to further increase his advantage of space and to prevent enemy's castling. Black prepares an attack with its pawns on the queenside, but because of White's powerful attack in center it will be obliged to quit soon this plan.

15. Rh1-h4! Nc5-a4

White makes again a strategic move. He refuses to take the pawn on h7 and thus to regain the sacrificed pawn in the opening, because this would allow Black to make castling. White move his rook on h4 to supra defend the c4-pawn and then to can participate together with bishop on g4 in attack of black king.

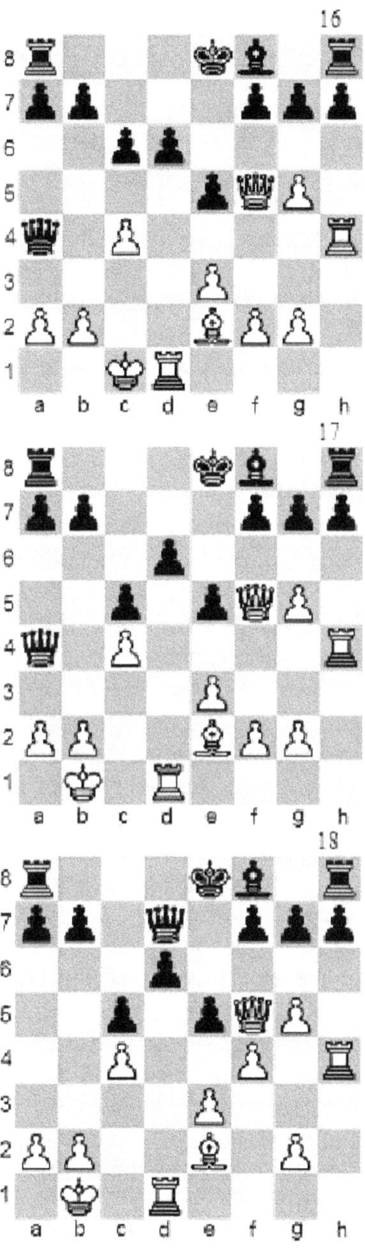

16. Nc3xa4 Qb4xa4

White eliminates from play one of the two black attacking pieces and Black cannot quickly bring other pieces in attack. Its attack on a2-pawn can be easily rejected and then it will be forced to make just defending moves, having not time to counterattack. Its king is hard to defend, black pieces are inactive and still do not play together, due to loss of tempos in the opening.

17. Kc1-b1 c6-c5

Black's counterattack was finished without benefits, while White threatens the immediate breakage of central pawn chain that still defends the black king. Thus White is ready to play 18. f4 and then to attack with all his major pieces the black e5-pawn to capture it. Black prepares the withdrawal of queen on d7 to defend its king

18. f2-f4 Qa4-d7

White begins in good time the attack on opponent's defensive device. Black proposes exchange of its inactive queen on the very active white queen and thus to decrease the pressure and make the castling. White refuses exchange and withdraws the queen on e4. Black still can't castle because follows Be2-g4 and White wins.

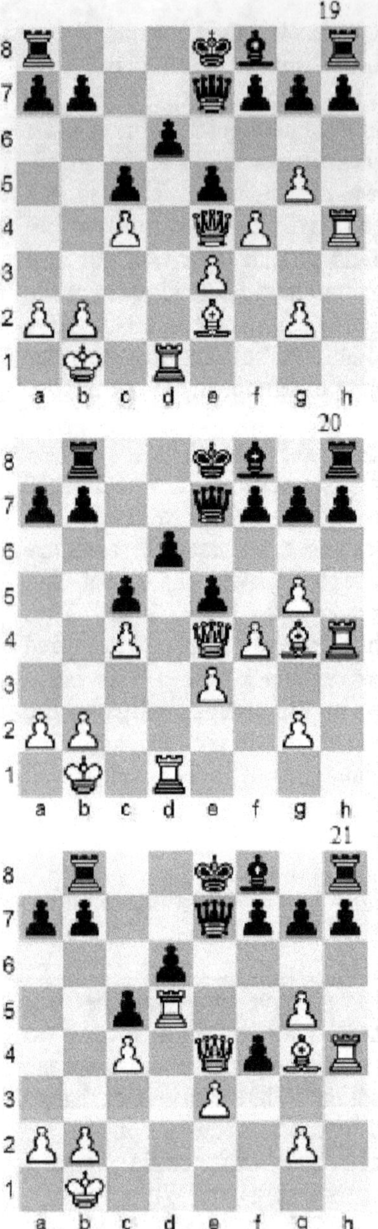

19. Qf5-e4! Qd7-e7

On e4 white Queen is as active as on f5 and continues to maintain the pressure in center. Black defends temporarily the e5-pawn and then wants to exchange this pawn no longer tenable because White can attack it with a pawn and three major pieces. An also black queen leaves d7-square, avoiding to be captured after castling and White's move Bg4.

20. Be2-g4! Ra8-b8

The g4-bishop takes definitely under control the h3-c8 diagonal, prevents opponent's queenside castling and restricts the mobility in defense of black pieces. Black abandons the intention of castling and wants to support b-pawn's advancement in order to attack white c4-pawn and open the b-file. But Black will not have enough time for this operation.

21. Rd1-d5! e5xf4

The e5-pawn cannot be defended and therefore Black exchanges it for white pawn on f4 and offers again the exchange of queens. It has solved the problem with defense of the e5-pawn, but the opening of f-file creates on f7 a new critical black weakness very hard to defend because now White can attack it with all his pieces, except king.

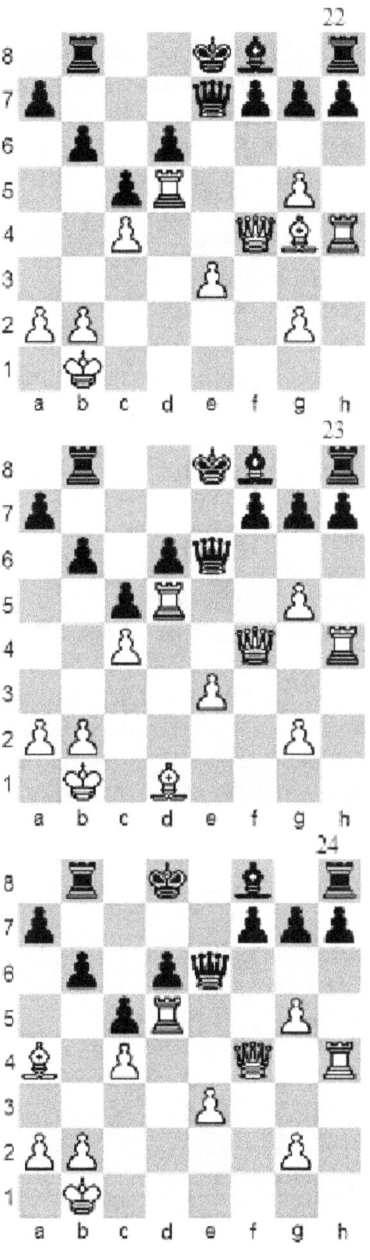

22. Qe4xf4 b7-b6

White refuses again the exchange of queens, captures the f4-pawn and begins immediately the attack on f7-pawn. His plan is to continue this attack moving the d5-rook on f5, the h4-rook on f1 and the bishop on d5. To these four attacks Black can respond in good time with three defenders only: with king on e8, queen on g6 and b-rook on b7.

23. Bg4-d1! Qe7-e6

White bishop has done its duty on kingside. Now it is preparing to occupy with tempo central field d5, where it will contribute to attack on both sides, exploiting light squares weaknesses in Black's position. Black cannot prevent this maneuver without major risks and releases e7-square for its bishop or for the b8-rook to attack the white e3-pawn.

24. Bd1-a4+ Ke8-d8 (see D. 24)
25. Rd5-f5 Rb8-b7
26. Ba4-c6 Rb7-e7

During the time spent by White to bring his bishop on c6 in its way to d5, Black finally mobilizes two major pieces to a double attack on white e3-pawn. But this attack brings no advantage because Black cannot support it in the absence of additional pieces available.

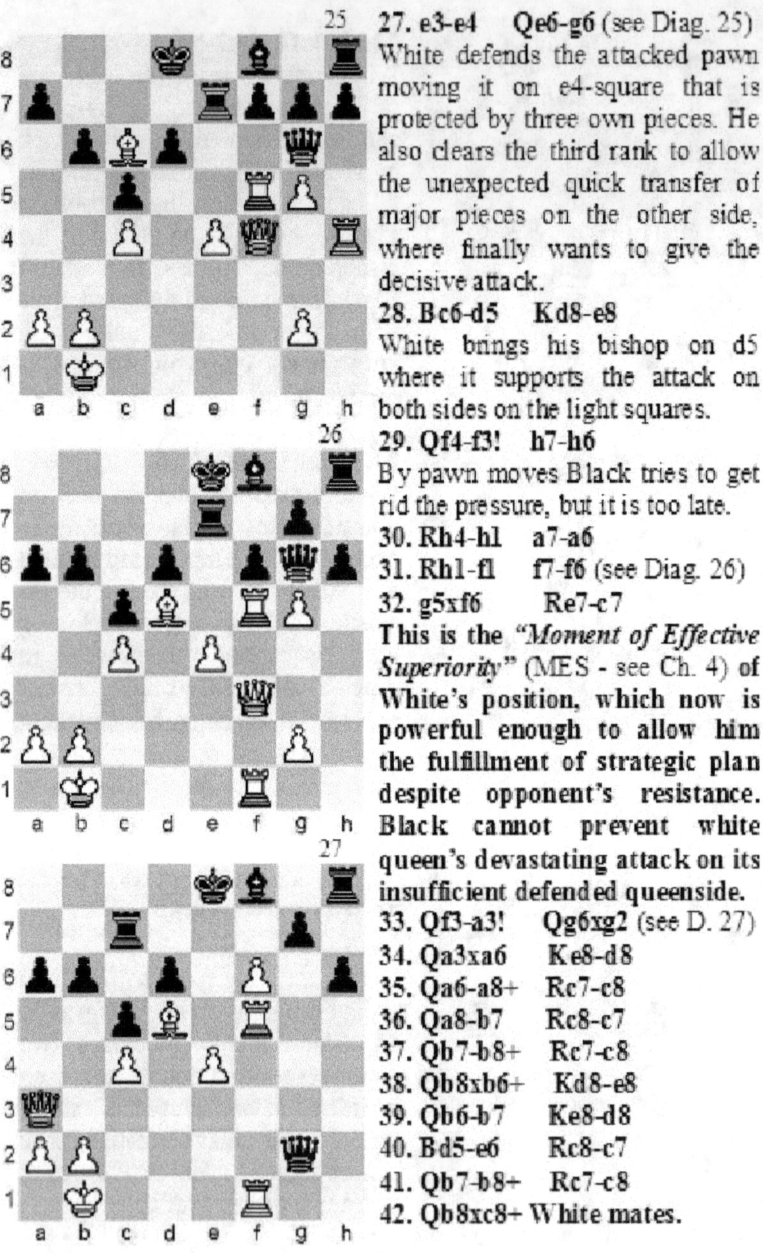

27. e3-e4 Qe6-g6 (see Diag. 25)
White defends the attacked pawn moving it on e4-square that is protected by three own pieces. He also clears the third rank to allow the unexpected quick transfer of major pieces on the other side, where finally wants to give the decisive attack.

28. Bc6-d5 Kd8-e8
White brings his bishop on d5 where it supports the attack on both sides on the light squares.

29. Qf4-f3! h7-h6
By pawn moves Black tries to get rid the pressure, but it is too late.

30. Rh4-h1 a7-a6
31. Rh1-f1 f7-f6 (see Diag. 26)
32. g5xf6 Re7-c7
This is the *"Moment of Effective Superiority"* (MES - see Ch. 4) **of White's position, which now is powerful enough to allow him the fulfillment of strategic plan despite opponent's resistance. Black cannot prevent white queen's devastating attack on its insufficient defended queenside.**

33. Qf3-a3! Qg6xg2 (see D. 27)
34. Qa3xa6 Ke8-d8
35. Qa6-a8+ Rc7-c8
36. Qa8-b7 Rc8-c7
37. Qb7-b8+ Rc7-c8
38. Qb8xb6+ Kd8-e8
39. Qb6-b7 Ke8-d8
40. Bd5-e6 Rc8-c7
41. Qb7-b8+ Rc7-c8
42. Qb8xc8+ White mates.

Summary

From the first seven tempos Black has spent five for nothing, i.e. without bringing into play new pieces and without tracking a right strategic plan. The g8-knight has left board without bringing any advantage in Black's position and the capture of "poisoned" d4-pawn does not compensate its losses of tempo suffered for this purpose just when they are less desirable.

After 17 moves, one single black piece is active: the queen on a4 and king cannot be protected by castling on queenside. White has already finished the opening and has four active pieces and four pawns ready to attack in center and on kingside. All his pieces have enough space available to play and may well cooperate with each other immediately in the attack against the opponent's king.

Until the 33th move Black hardly resisted, but it had to give back the pawn captured in the opening and its king position is still very vulnerable. To move away black queen from Black's defensive device, White had sacrificed the g2-pawn and started the matting attack with his queen against Black's king through queenside, poorly defended by a single piece: the c7 rook.

Game 2

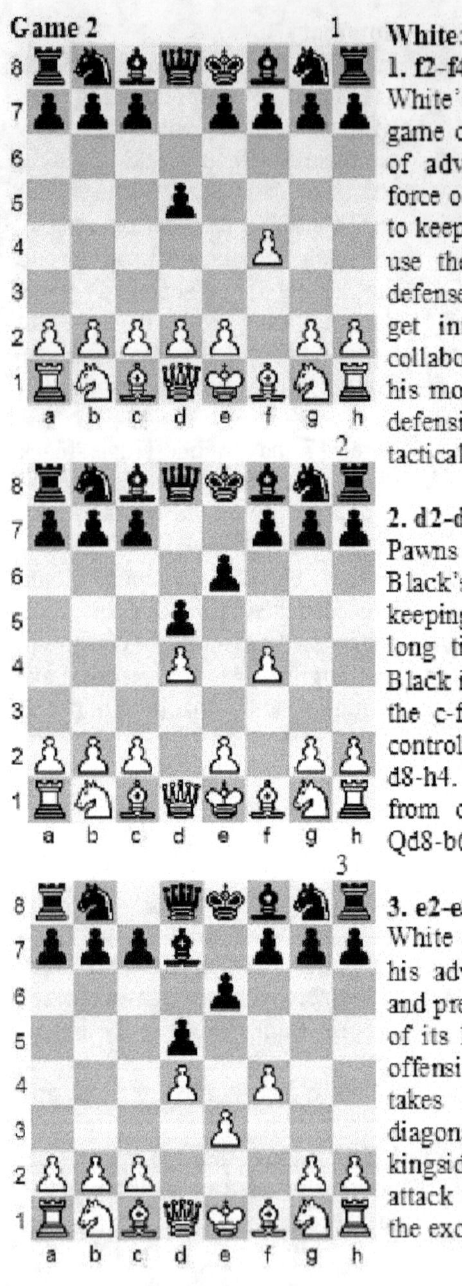

White: C. M. Black: Computer

1. f2-f4 d7-d5

White's strategic plan consists of game closing to decrease mobility of adverse bishops and increase force of own knights, that he wants to keep as much as possible and to use them in breaking of Black's defense device. His pieces must get into the game quickly and collaborate with one another. All his moves must have a quadruple defensive-offensive and strategic-tactical character.

2. d2-d4! e7-e6

Pawns on d4 and f4 do not allow Black's liberating move e7-e5, keeping the center closed for a long time, until the final attack. Black intends to move c7-c5, open the c-file and allow its queen to control the diagonals d8-a5 and d8-h4. If White moves the bishop from c1, Black intends to move Qd8-b6 with attack on b2-pawn.

3. e2-e3 Bc8-d7

White consolidates the defense of his advanced d4- and f4- pawns and prepares the entering into play of its light squared bishop on an offensive position in d3, where it takes the control of important diagonal b1-h7 for future White's kingside attack. Black aims to attack on queenside and prepares the exchange of its bad bishop.

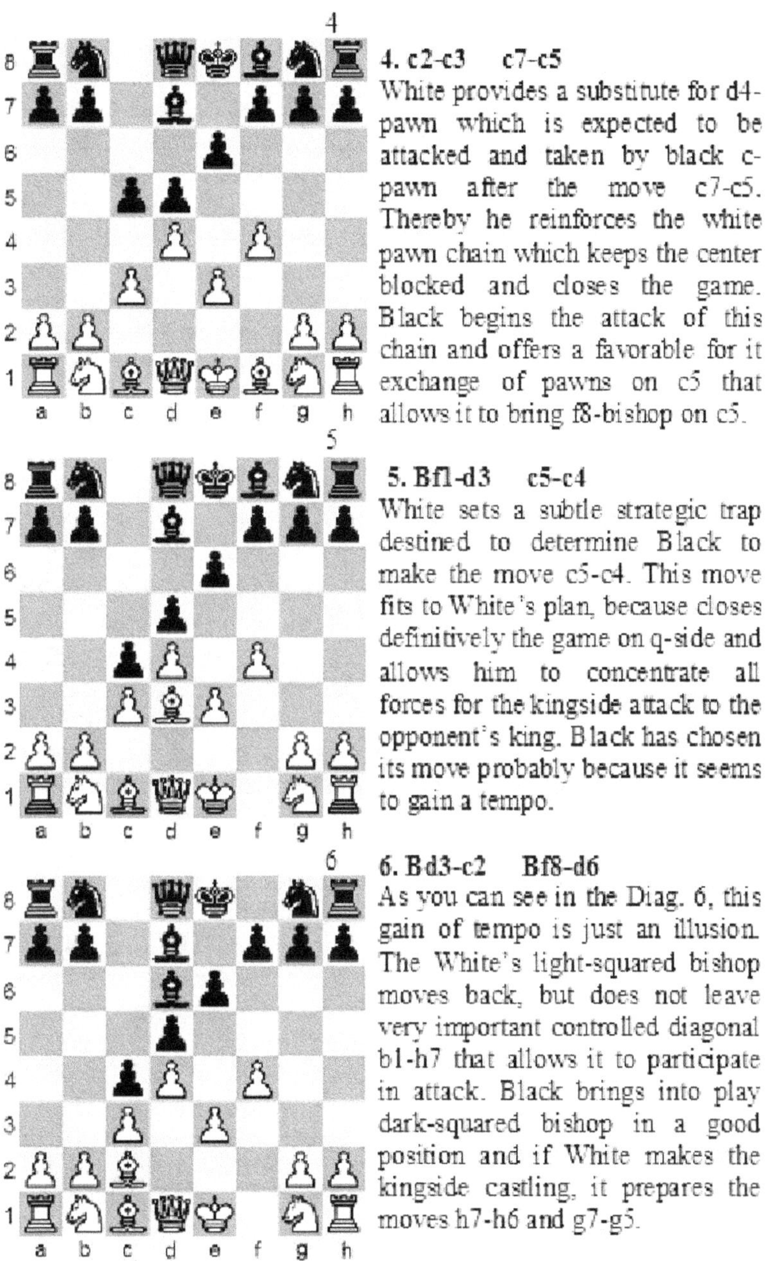

4. c2-c3 c7-c5

White provides a substitute for d4-pawn which is expected to be attacked and taken by black c-pawn after the move c7-c5. Thereby he reinforces the white pawn chain which keeps the center blocked and closes the game. Black begins the attack of this chain and offers a favorable for it exchange of pawns on c5 that allows it to bring f8-bishop on c5.

5. Bf1-d3 c5-c4

White sets a subtle strategic trap destined to determine Black to make the move c5-c4. This move fits to White's plan, because closes definitively the game on q-side and allows him to concentrate all forces for the kingside attack to the opponent's king. Black has chosen its move probably because it seems to gain a tempo.

6. Bd3-c2 Bf8-d6

As you can see in the Diag. 6, this gain of tempo is just an illusion. The White's light-squared bishop moves back, but does not leave very important controlled diagonal b1-h7 that allows it to participate in attack. Black brings into play dark-squared bishop in a good position and if White makes the kingside castling, it prepares the moves h7-h6 and g7-g5.

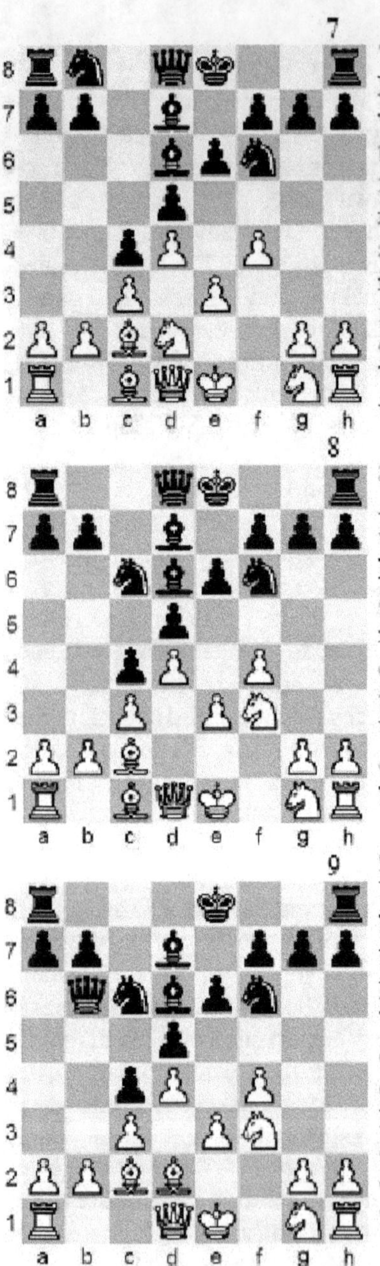

7. Nb1-d2 Ng8-f6
Now White's position has no weaknesses which need to spend time for their defense, so he can fully use all time and other resources only for preparing his attack on kingside. The b1-knight is moving towards this side and frees square b1 for the withdrawal of the light-squared bishop. Then White intends to move Qd1-c2 with double attack on h7-pawn.

8. Nd2-f3 Nb8-c6
All White's pieces have free way to support the attack against Black's king, except a1-rook and c1-bishop which are kept on the initial position to ensure the defense of queenside. To gain a tempo for quick development, White intends to renounce of castling. As long as the center is blocked, castling is not necessary.

9. Bc1-d2! Qd8-b6
White intentionally left defenseless b2-pawn to attract black queen on b6, away from its king. Black hopes that this move will force White to make an inactive move to defend b2-pawn. Also it brings the queen into the play and allows its king to make the queenside castling. But this move can be exploited by White because blocks the advancement of black b-pawn.

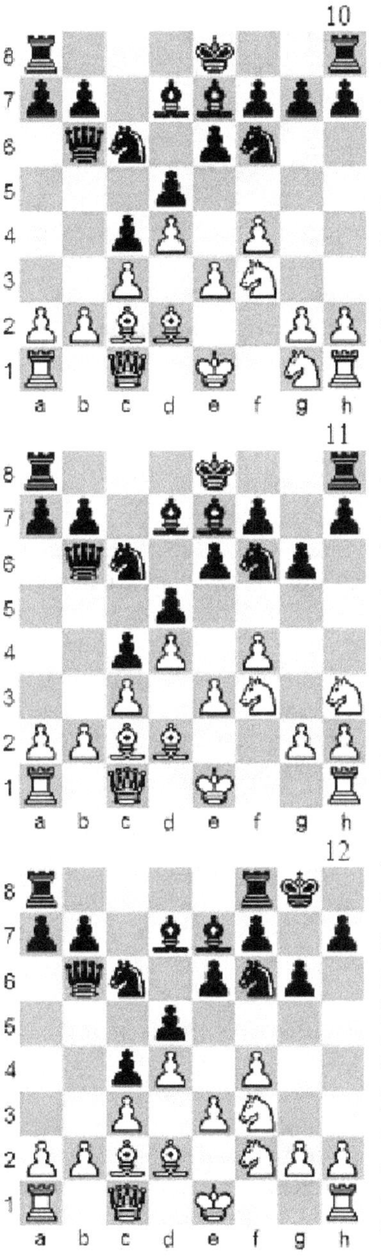

10. Qd1-c1! Bd6-e7

White doesn't defend the b2 pawn with rook on b1 because he wants to keep the possibility of queenside castling when this will be necessary to a quick entry of a1-rook into the play to support the attack. On c1 queen strengthens so much the White's queenside that Black is completely discouraged from attacking in this area

11. Ng1-h3! g7-g6

White wants to bring the g1-knight through h3 on f2, to prepare the beginning of his pawn storm against enemy's king with move g2-g4 followed by h2-h4.and h4-h5. All his pieces are placed on squares from which they can trigger almost immediately the attack in a perfect collaboration between them.

12. Nh3-f2 0 – 0

With this move, preparation of White's attack was ended. His two neighboring knights offer many possibilities for cooperation with pawns in front of them and with other pieces, except with d2-bishop that defends its king. However, Black has chosen to do the kingside castling, because on queenside it has considered most dangerous White's attack which begins with move b2-b3.

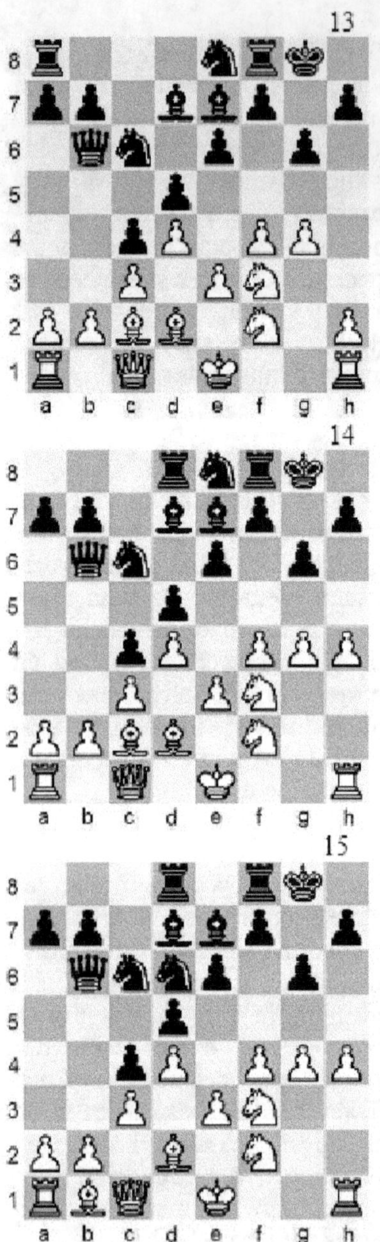

13. g2-g4! Nf6-e8

White's attack has started with multiple threats, and from this moment Black has definitely lost possibility of taking over the management of the game. To defend the king, Black uses the pawns in front of it and its two bishops, and intends to try a counterattack with move f7-f5 followed by moves Ke8-d6 and Kd6-e4.

14. h2-h4 Ra8-d8

White continues to grow almost unhindered the strategic pressure on kingside. Black is trying to bring a8-rook in support of king's defense, but this intention is very hard to accomplish among its cramped and practically lacking of useful mobility pieces. Black's bishops are crowded and tangle the play of the other black pieces.

15. Bc2-b1 Ne8-d6

White prepares to move the queen on c2 where it will continue to defend b2-pawn and at the same time to increases pressure on b1-h7 very important diagonal for final battle. Black is trying to transfer the d6-knight on e4 if f2-knight will advance, in order to interrupt the double very dangerous action of b1-bishop and c2-queen along this diagonal.

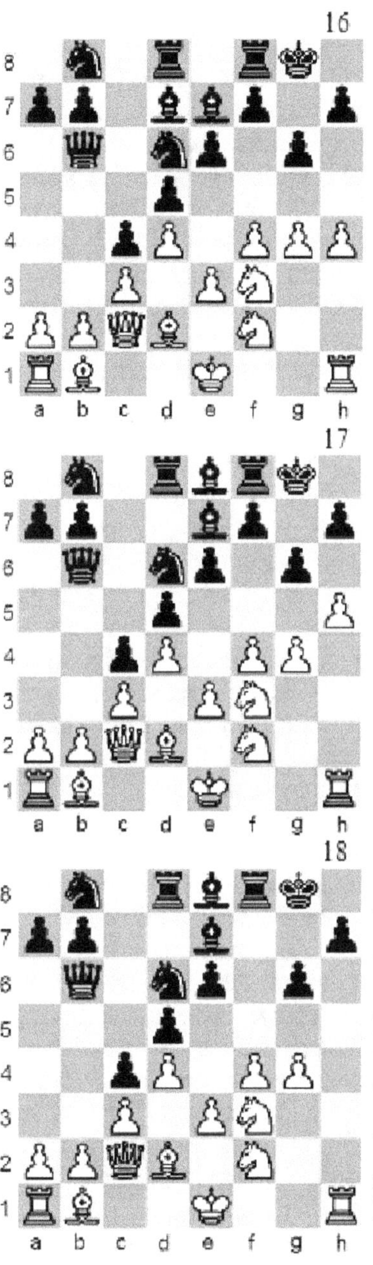

16. Qc1-c2 Nc6-b8

White prepares breakage of pawn chain defending opposing king with the move 17. h4-h5 and opening of h-file for h1-rook. Black sees that c6-knight doesn't participate in any attack or defense action and this is the reason why it decides to bring this piece in defense on kingside, moving it first on b8 and then on d7 and f6 or f8 to cover h7- or g6- pawn.

17. h4-h5 Bd7-e8

After this White's move, the breaking of Black's pawn chain that defends its king and opening of h-file for h1 rook are inevitable. Black has nothing to do but to defend once with its bishop on e8 the g6-pawn, one of the most important targets of opponent's attack. The exchange of pawns on h5 is unacceptable for Black; also exchange on g6 isn't it favorable.

18. h5xg6 f7xg6

White has already managed to open h-file for his major pieces attack against black king. The two pawns h7 and g6 are strongly attacked by three white pieces and defended by two black pieces only, one of which being even the king. White may further increase the number of his attacking pieces and Black's position will collapse.

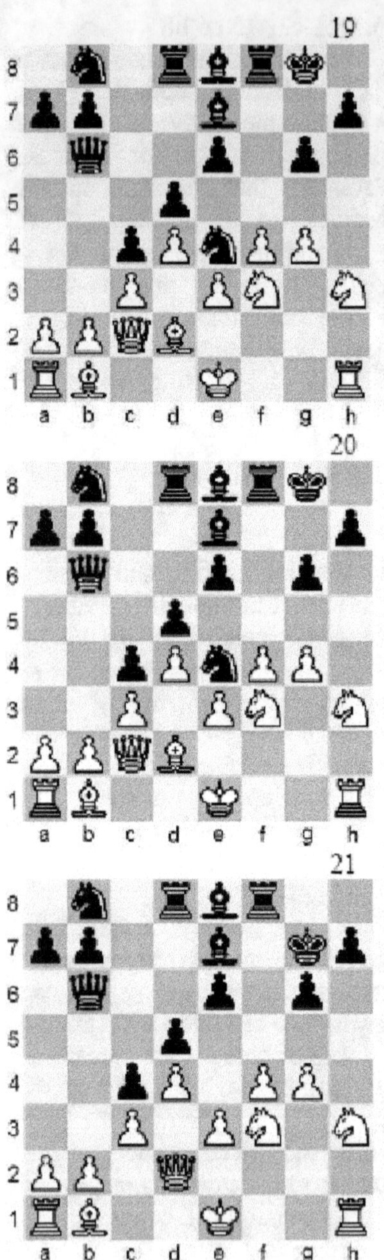

19. Nf2-h3 Nd6-e4

For his attack on g6 and h7 pawns, White wants to bring knights on e5 and g5. Black knight occupies a central square on e4, but it will not be able to keep this advantageous position because is not sufficiently supported by other black pieces and can be captured by b1-bishop. Therefore Black will be forced to exchange it for d2-bishop, move which favors White.

20. Qc2-c1 Ne4xd2

White moves c2 queen to allow b1-bishop capture the opponent's knight infiltrated between his pieces. Black cannot accept the exchange on e4, because creates there a weak black pawn for whose defense should displace a piece of defense of own king. He takes the d2 bishop hoping to weaken the white pawn chain.

21. Qc1xd2 Kg8-g7

The exchange of minor pieces made by Black on d2 favors White because on this square his queen still defends b2-pawn and prepares to participate in the attack moving to h2 and creating thus a battery of major pieces on open h-file. Black's king move to g7 to clear the way for f8-rook to reach the h8-square where it will defend the weak h7-pawn.

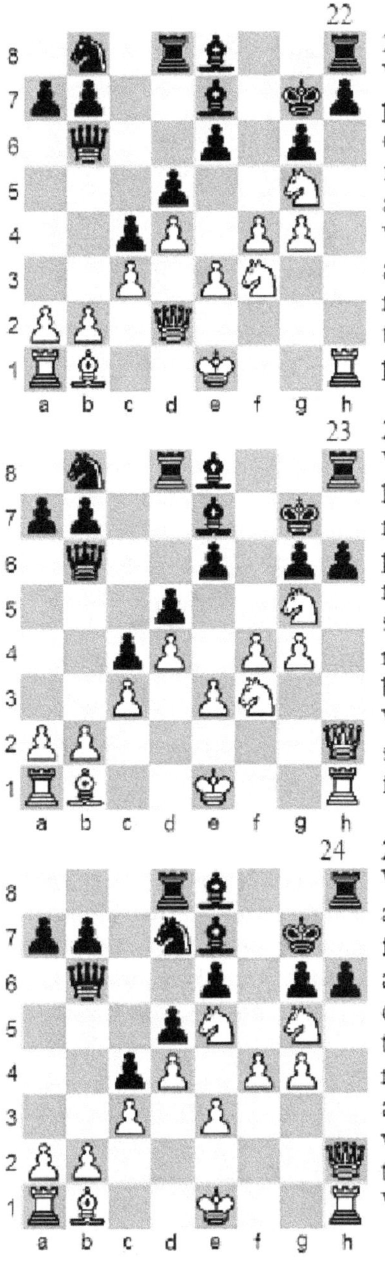

22. Nh3-g5 Rf8-h8

White continues to attack the h7-pawn bringing one of his knights on g5 and offering to exchange it for black e7-bishop. If Black accepts this exchange on g5, then White brings there his other knight and the pressure on kingside does not weaken. Black doesn't accept this exchange and defends the h7-pawn with h8-rook.

23. Qd2-h2 h7-h6

White strengthens the attack on h7-pawn creating a battery of major pieces on h-file. Black protects its weak attacked pawn moving it on h6 square for now sufficiently defended. But this move wakens the g6-square which becomes the main target of White's attack. Conquering this square, White will decide in his favor the fate of the game.

24. Nf3-e5 Nb8-d7

White immediately starts the attack on g6-square with his knight from e5. The g6-pawn is already attacked by the bishop from b1 and can still be attacked by bringing the white queen on c2. Black moves its b8-knight on d7 attacking the white knight on e5 which it wants to eliminate from the game in order to weaken White's attack

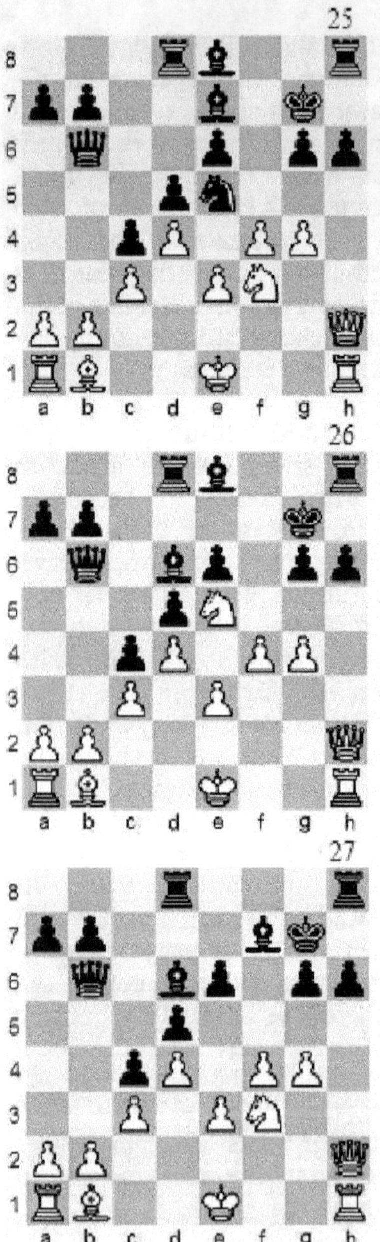

25. Ng5-f3 Nd7xe5
White defends immediately attacked e5-knight with his other knight, to replace it if will be taken by black d7-knight. So White still maintains the multiple attacks on g6-square, viewing it conquest. Not having other better move, Black accepts the exchange of knights on e5, hoping to exchange then the second white knight for its dark-lighted bishop from e7.

26. Nf3xe5 Be7-d6
Black wants to eliminate White's e5-knight, hoping thus to decrease pressure in center and on kingside. Black also obviously seeks to gain time to mobilize pieces on active positions for defense and to restore the balance of forces on kingside. In addition, Black is interested to exchange its bishop for the more active white knight.

27. Ne5-f3! Ne8-f7
White doesn't accept the exchange of pieces on e5 and temporarily withdraws the knight on f3, from where it can attack again g6-square on e5 or on h4. Black's dark-squared bishop will not stop this new attack, because it cannot control simultaneously both e5- and h4- squares. Black allows d8-rook to participate in defense of g- and h-files.

28. Qh2-c2 a7-a5

Black understands that on kingside the battle will soon be lost and tries to start a counterattack on the other side. But there White has no weaknesses to defend immediately against this counterattack and can bring his knight in attack with a devastating effect on Black's defending device which will fall after a few moves.

29. Nf3-h4 g6-g5

Black cannot defend g6-square and then advances the pawn from this square to g5, where temporarily it seems to be enough defended. But after this move, entire b1-h7 diagonal belongs to White and allows him more possibilities to attack the black king and its defenders. For this reason, Black has no defenses against all White's threats.

30. Nh4-g6! g5xf4

With this move, White begins to reap the fruits of his strategic plan followed from the start up of this game. He kept up the play closed and a knight for the final coup in collaboration with all his other pieces, except the king. To weaken pressure, not having other better move, Black is forced to accept the exchange of its h8-rook for White's knight and two pawns.

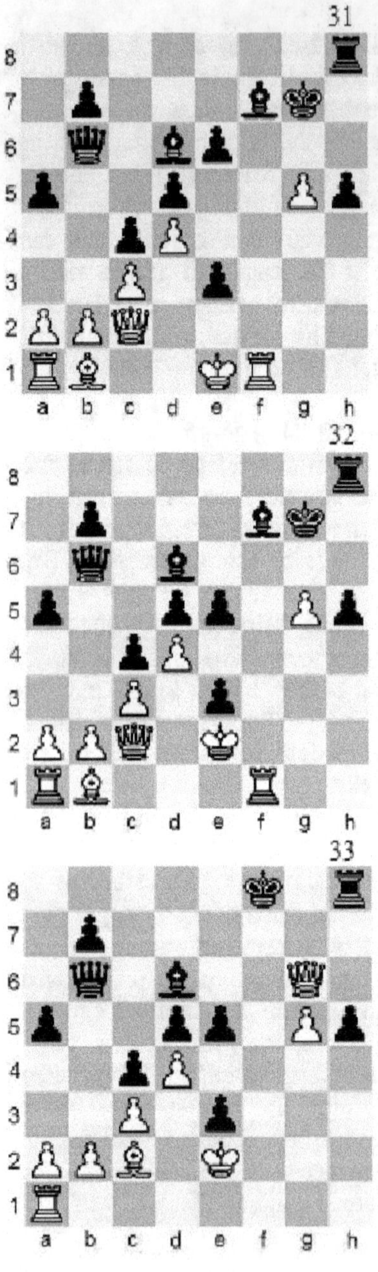

31. Ng6xh8 Rd8xh8
32. g4-g5 h6-h5
33. Rh1-f1! f4xe3 (see Diag. 31)
White attacks the black f4 pawn that in the next moves can be defended twice only, while he can easy attack it three times. The advancement of this weak f4-pawn also is not helping, so Black decides to capture with it the white e3-pawn. But this opens f-file that White will quickly exploit.

34. Ke1-e2! e6-e5 (see Diag. 32)
White makes now a lingeringly prepared move with quadruple active character (strategic and tactical, defensive and offensive) that quickly decides the fate of the game in his favor. Black wrongly appreciates that white pressure has now disappeared, even with some chances for it to win and that it is time to counterattack in center. In reality White reached MES (see Ch. 4). It followed:
35. Rf1xf7+!! Kg7xf7
36. Qc2-g6+ Rf7-f8
37. Bb1-c2!! (see Diag. 33)
Again a White's move with quadruple character after that Black will be checkmated soon:
37 ... Qb6xb2 What else?
38. Ra1-f1+ Kf8-e7
39. Rf1-f7+ Ke7-e8
40. Qg6-e6+ Ke8-d8
41. Qe6-d7+ White mates.

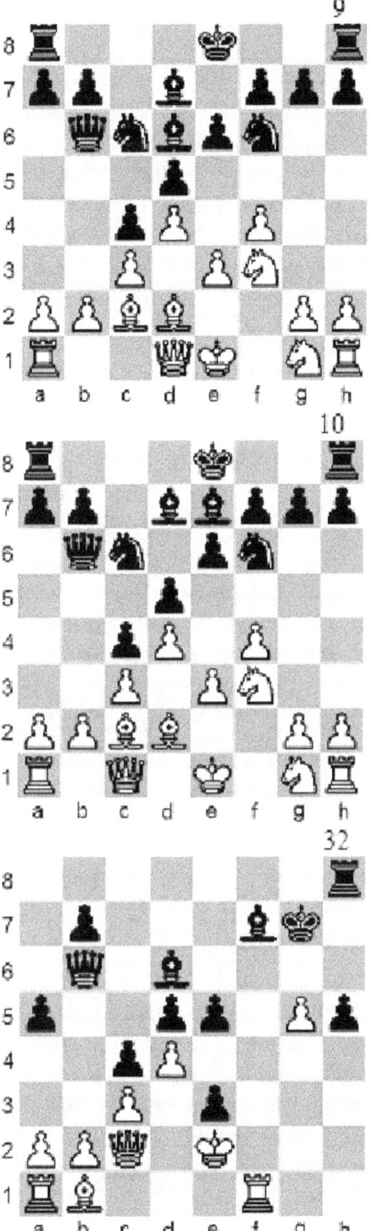

Summary

As you can see in Diag. 9, after nine moves Black's position seems to be better. Black has three pieces only in the starting position, while White has five. Black can castle on both sides, while White cannot do it on any side. In reality, White's position is much more promising, because all his pieces are behind pawns and they can collaborate better to attack on both sides.

10. Qd1-c1! Bd6-e7

While the White's move has a purpose in accordance with his strategic plan and contributes to its accomplishment, Black's move is a step back which loses a tempo and clearly reveals its lack of strategic plan. Black has not yet decided on which side to do castling. It waits to appear a weakness on one of sides in White's position to castle on the other side and then to attack it.

After 34 moves it has reached the position in Diag.32. Black's pieces are scattered on the board without collaborations, while white pieces are all focused to attack on kingside and with the move **35. Rf1xf7!!** White begins to realize his positional superiority. A very instructive game about how to play and win against computer using the scientific management.

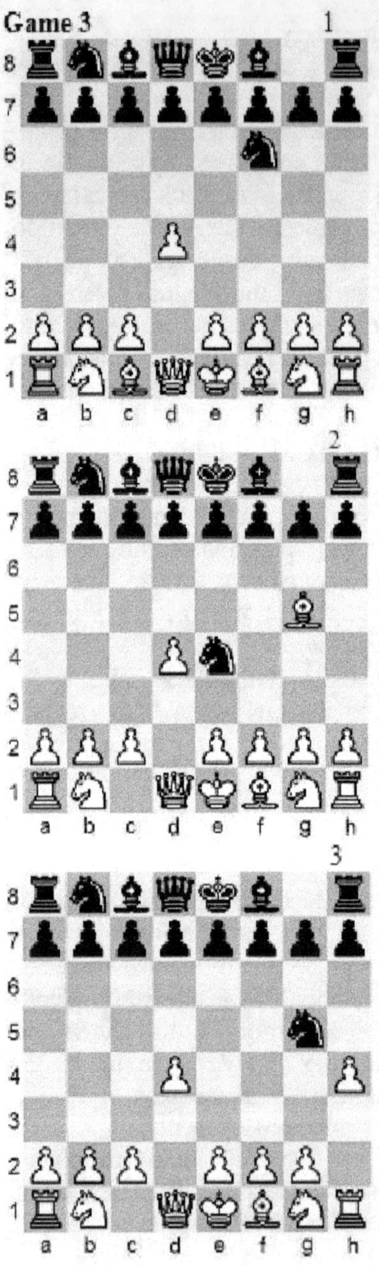

White: C.M. Black: Computer

1. d2-d4 Ng8-f6

The computer has no imagination and consequently cannot conceive new strategic plans. But he quickly inventories adverse pieces that can be attacked or captured and attacks them directly or by combinations of several moves. White's strategic plan is to close the game in the center and on queenside and then to attack on the other side.

2. Bc1-g5 Nf6-e4

Black's attacking move is typical for its style of play: almost always it attacks promptly the opponent's piece which can be captured next move, trying thus to take or keep the initiative in the game. But now this second move with the same piece in the opening of game loses a tempo in developing of pieces required to prepare efficiently the final decisive battle.

3. h2-h4! Ne4xg5

White chooses the move that best meets his strategic plan: increases activity of two pieces on kingside: the h-pawn and the rook from h1 opening the h-file for it. If he had retired bishop, he would lose a tempo. Also to the loss of a tempo would have resulted if White would have defended bishop with the knight or with the queen after Black's moves 3...Nxg5 and 4...h6.

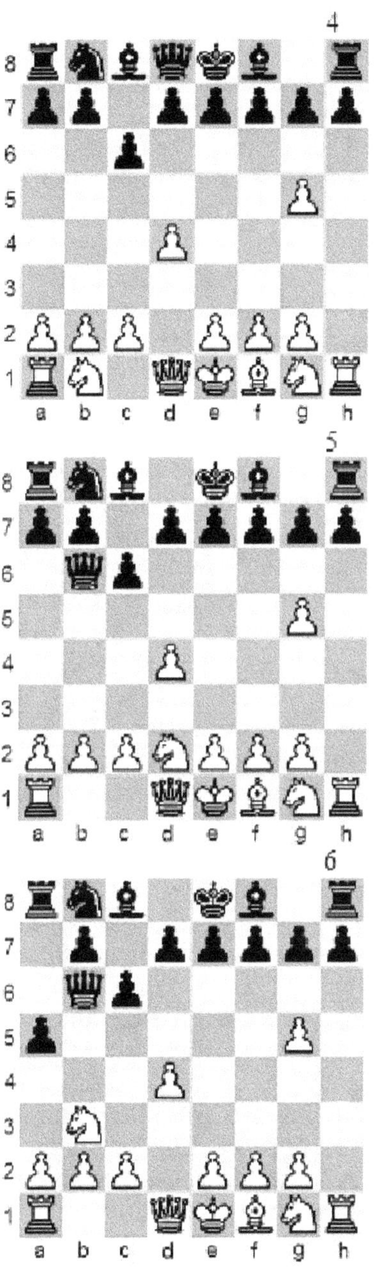

4. h4xg5 c7-c6

Black "sees" an undefended white piece: the b2 pawn, and prepares its attack with queen on b6, in order to delay White's queenside castling and to take the initiative in the game. Black's move clearly reveals again its almost exclusive tactical play method mentioned above. The same method of play we meet in Black's moves number 13, 20 and 21.

5. Nb1-d2 Qd8-b6

Black queen attacks at the same time the b2 and d4 white pawns, but its early entry into the play before minor pieces cannot be considered a good move because this isolated attack can easily be rejected with opponent's moves which in addition contribute to his rapid development of minor pieces required in the opening phase of the game.

6. Nd2-b3 a7-a5

According to its method, Black indirectly continuous the attack on b2 pawn, threatening to displace the knight that protects it on b3. But this Black's move does not put problems to its opponent, which have again a defensive move that bring into play new pieces, with advantage in development towards Black's position.

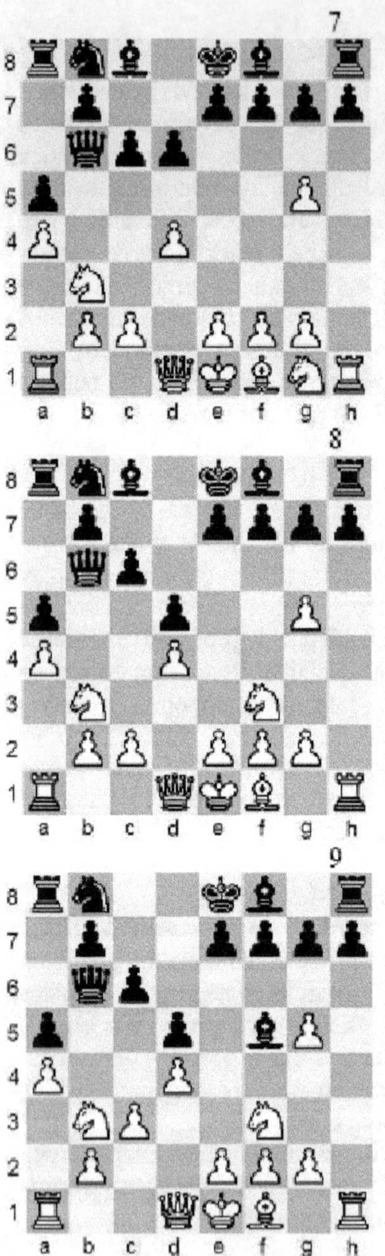

7

7. a2-a4 d7-d6

White blocks the advancement of black pawn on a-file, without weakening his position on queenside. Also he stops Black's attack on this side using moves which continue development of pieces according to his strategic plan. Black prepares game opening on queenside by advancing of its c-pawn and clears the way for c8 bishop on c8-h3 diagonal.

8

8. Ng1-f3 d6-d5

White brings into play a new piece and threats to place it on e5 from which Black cannot dislocate it without weakening its kingside position by move f7-f6. Black renounces to support advancement of c-pawn and moves again d-pawn losing a new tempo. The aim of this move is to prevent the White's move e2-e4 that would create a strong white center.

9

9. c2-c3 Bc8-f5

White prepares Qd1-c2 to attack the weak black pawn on h7 and to capture it. Also White's move prepares the queenside castling, his position being quite strong and without weaknesses easily to attack on this side. Black takes control of b1-h7 diagonal and thus stops for the moment the attack on weak pawn h7.

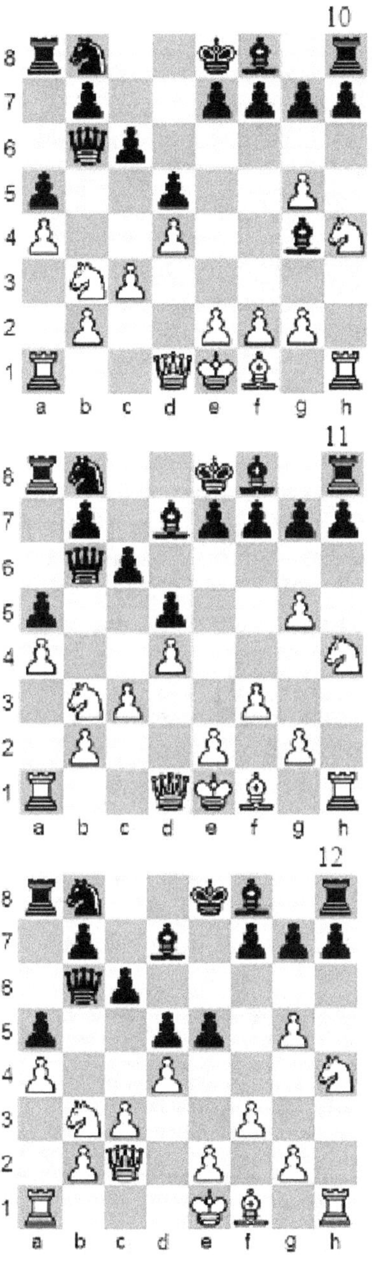

10. Nf3-h4 Bf5-g4

White moves the f3-knight on a position closer to the opposing king, in the same time driving out definitively the black bishop from the diagonal b1-h7 that he can use to attack with queen and with the bishop. On g4-square the black bishop doesn't have a stabile position and White can dislocate it with an active move and gaining a tempo in development.

11. f2-f3 Bg4-d7

Isolated incursions of Black's queen and of light-squared bishop have brought no advantage and its position has lagged behind in pieces development on active positions. After three moves the c8-bishop has reached o square where he could go after a single move. White has space advantage and can continue unimpeded his pieces development.

12. Qd1-c2 e7-e5!

Black's move proves its mastery to create complications that can be used in its advantage. Black tries to open the game, even with a pawn sacrifice. If White accepts the pawn sacrifice on e5, Black can activate its queen by move 13.,.. Qb6-e3 with double attack on e5 and g5, regaining the sacrificed pawn and improving its position.

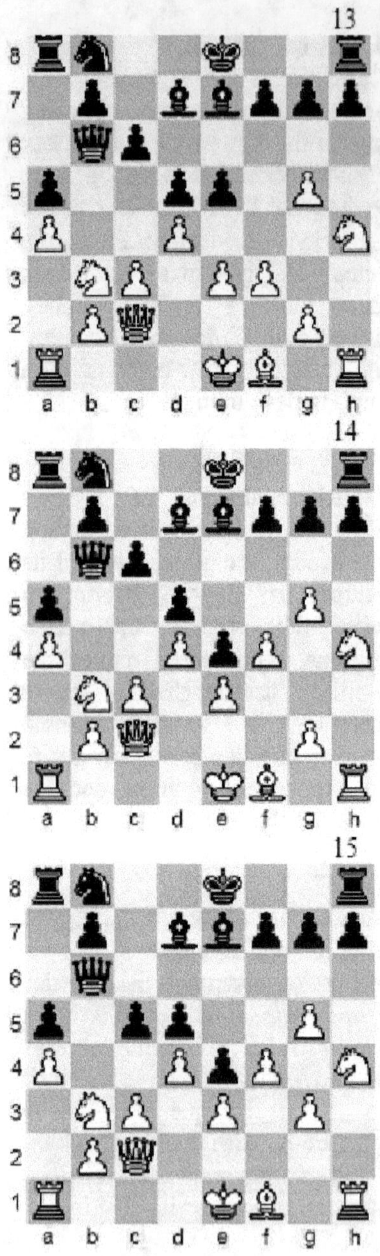

13. e2-e3 Bf8-e7

White doesn't accept the pawn sacrifice on e5 and continues to follow his strategic plan defending once more the d4 pawn, very important for keeping closed the center. Also he prepares the entry in battle of his bishop next move and the queen's moving to kingside to support the white pawns storm against black king.

14. f3-f4! e5-e4!

White begins at the right time the assault with his pawns and wants to open immediately one of e- or f-files for major pieces activation in attack. Black doesn't allow this, and permanently blocks the center and the White's pieces on b1-h7 diagonal, hoping thus to decrease pressure. But the connected two white f- and g- pawns become very dangerous.

15. g2-g3 c6-c5!

White extends his queen's access on the second rank and intends to move bishop on h3 to exchange it for the d7 bishop that defends Black's king. Black is used of the temporary decrease of pressure on its king's position and begins the attack on queenside, where it hopes to have some ways to balance the game activating of its minor pieces.

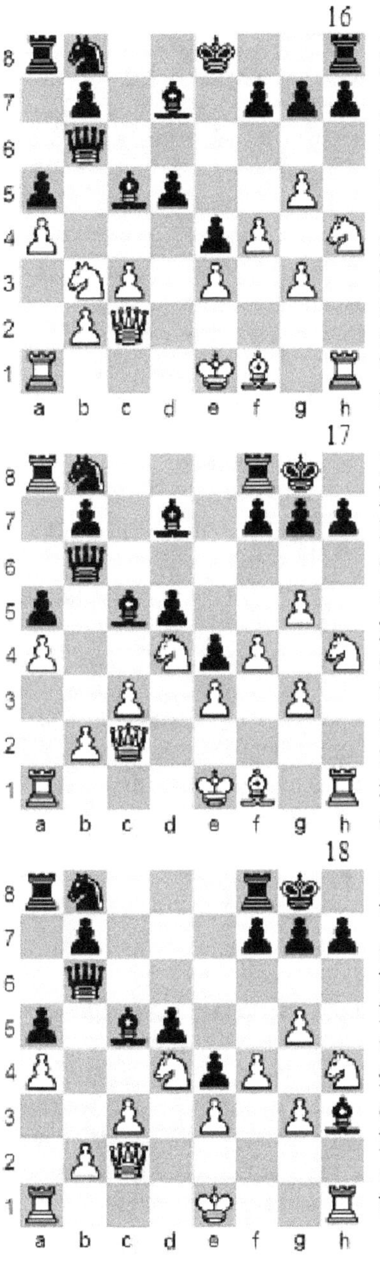

16. d4xc5 Be7xc5
White can't prevent the exchange of pawns on c5 or on d4, followed by the opening of c-file. In this situation, to maintain yet the center closed, he chooses to exchange pawns on c5 and instead of d4-pawn brings the knight from b3, attacked there by the black queen. Center remains closed and from White's position is eliminated the b3 weakness.

17. Nb3-d4! O-O
Black hurries now to make kingside castling and thus to bring on queenside the h8-rook to cooperate there with its other pieces in breaking opponent's defensive maneuvers. White seems to have lagged behind with a tempo and Black's position seems to be better. But the next few moves will demonstrate that this is only an illusion.

18. Bf1-h3! Bd7xh3
White forces the exchange of light-squares bishops, because his bishop has not yet a role and even hinders movement in attack, while the opponent's bishop is an important piece of defensive device of black king. In addition, h-rook advances on h3 and makes space for arrival behind of his brother from a1, gaining a tempo.

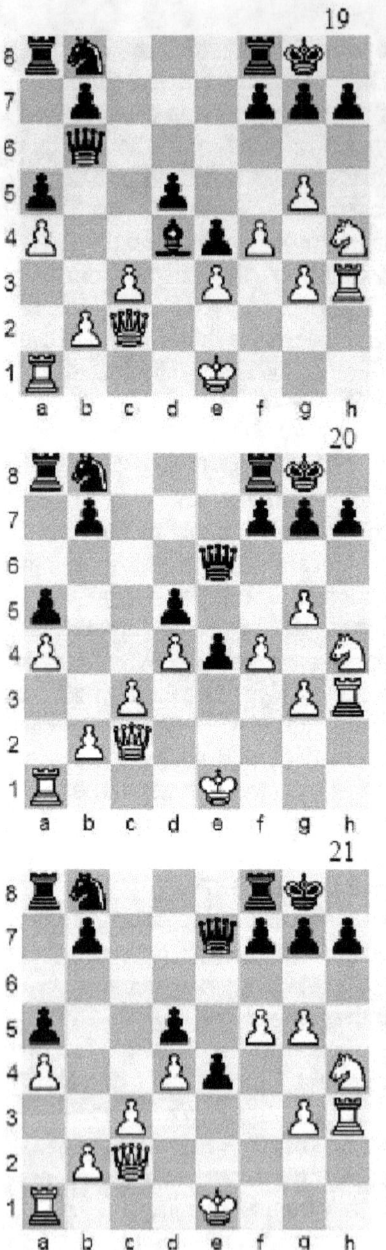

19. Rh1xh3 Bc5xd4
Black eliminates the central powerful white knight from d4 that threatens to participate in the attack against its king and creates a passed pawn on e-file which can advance and generate some problems for white in end-game phase. White considers that this passed pawn is not yet dangerous because it can be blocked easily with his king or queen on e3.

20. e3xd4 Qb6-e6
White takes the black bishop on d4 with e3-pawn and thus maintains the c-file semi-closed to not avoid Black to penetrate with queen and rooks in defending device of white king. As usual, Black attacks a defenseless opponent's piece, the h3-rook, but this attack can easily be rejected with a move that continues to execute the White's strategic plan.

21. f4-f5! Qe6-e7
Black makes again a move that can easily be rejected with a move which continues to execute White's strategic plan. But this time, White will have to avoid a small trap: if to defend the g5-pawn he moves 22. Qd2?, then Black responds 22...e3!, g5-pawn will be captured and force of White's attack will decrease.

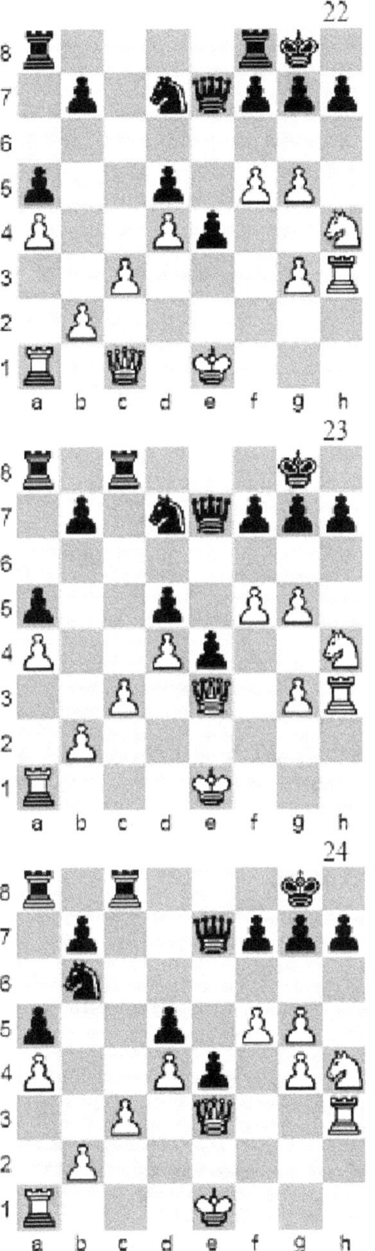

22. Qc2-c1! Nb8-d7
Through d7 and b6 Black wants to bring b8-knight to c4-square from which it can attack b2-pawn, the base of pawn chain that ensures the good opponent's defense on queenside. Also, from there this black knight can move on d6 to participate in defense of kingside where it is clear that will be the decisive battle. Black expects White's long castling.

23. Qc1-e3! Rf8-c8
White makes a strategic move that permanently blocks the center and leaves the way free for bringing a1-rook on kingside to participate in the final attack. His king is safe behind the blocked center and does not intend to castle. Black wants to bring f8-rook on 6th rank to participate in defense of its king against White's threats.

24. g3-g4 Nd7-b6
Black threatens to move 25...Nc4 attacking with tempo at the same time two white pieces: the queen and the b2-pawn. Now White can defend itself moving 25. b3 and creating thus a new weakness on b3-square, but still at least a few tempos an enemy's piece will not attack it due the lack of time created by the strong White's offensive on the other side.

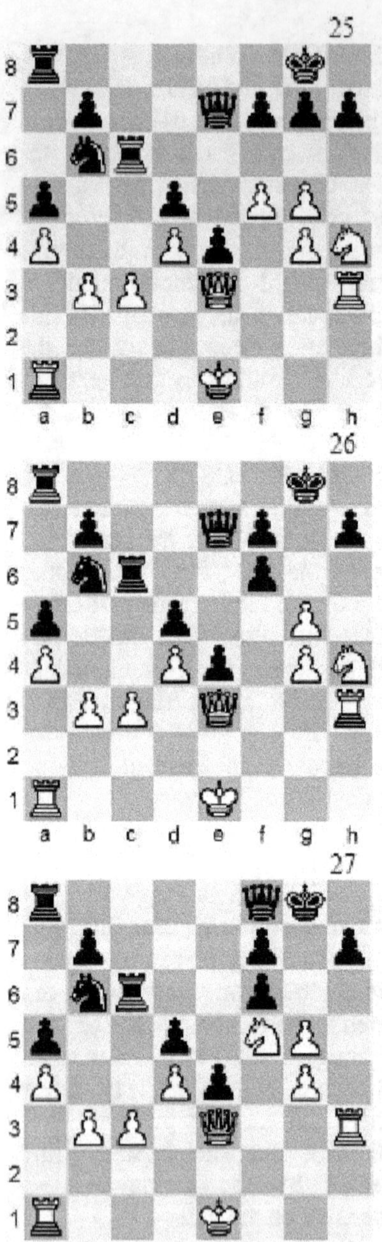

25. b2-b3 Rc8-c6
Black transfers c-rook on 6th rank to prevent the white pawn storm against defensive device of black king that will begin next move. But this storm cannot be prevent, because White's position reached the *Moment of Effective Superiority* (MES - see Ch. 4) in which this positional superiority can be transformed tactically in a big advantage that ensures the victory.

26. f5-f6!! g7xf6
White makes an unexpected sacrifice to break the chain of pawns which still maintains a temporary defense for opposing king and to allow then the assault of all white pieces yet mobilized in zone and the decisive coup with a1-rook prepared for this. Forced moves that follow cannot allow a sufficient defense for exposed black king.

27. Nh4-f5! Qe7-f8.
For the successful continuation of the attack, at the right time White makes with tempo an important move in order to dislocate the black queen from e7 where it defends f6-pawn. Also he opens the h-file to create a white rook battery and prepares a double attack with knight on e7.(see move 30. Nf5-e7 in Diag. 30).

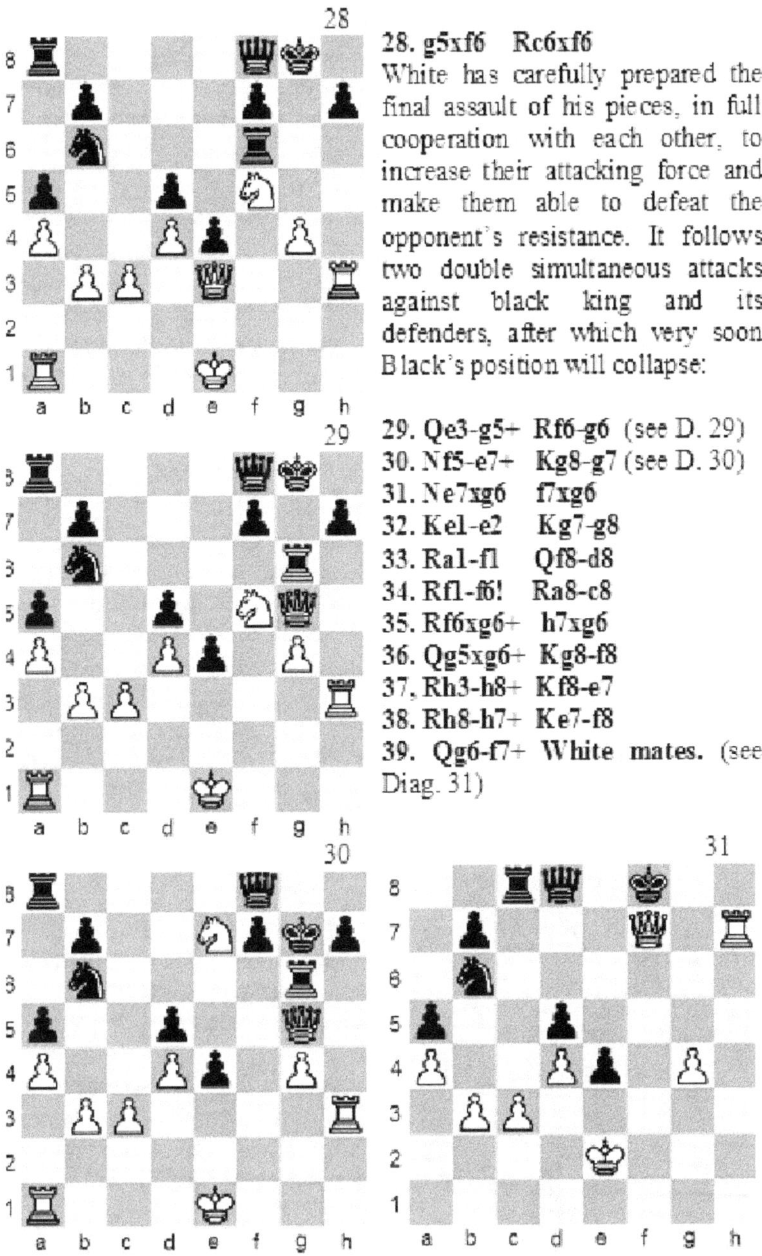

28. g5xf6 Rc6xf6

White has carefully prepared the final assault of his pieces, in full cooperation with each other, to increase their attacking force and make them able to defeat the opponent's resistance. It follows two double simultaneous attacks against black king and its defenders, after which very soon Black's position will collapse:

29. Qe3-g5+ Rf6-g6 (see D. 29)
30. Nf5-e7+ Kg8-g7 (see D. 30)
31. Ne7xg6 f7xg6
32. Ke1-e2 Kg7-g8
33. Ra1-f1 Qf8-d8
34. Rf1-f6! Ra8-c8
35. Rf6xg6+ h7xg6
36. Qg5xg6+ Kg8-f8
37. Rh3-h8+ Kf8-e7
38. Rh8-h7+ Ke7-f8
39. Qg6-f7+ White mates. (see Diag. 31)

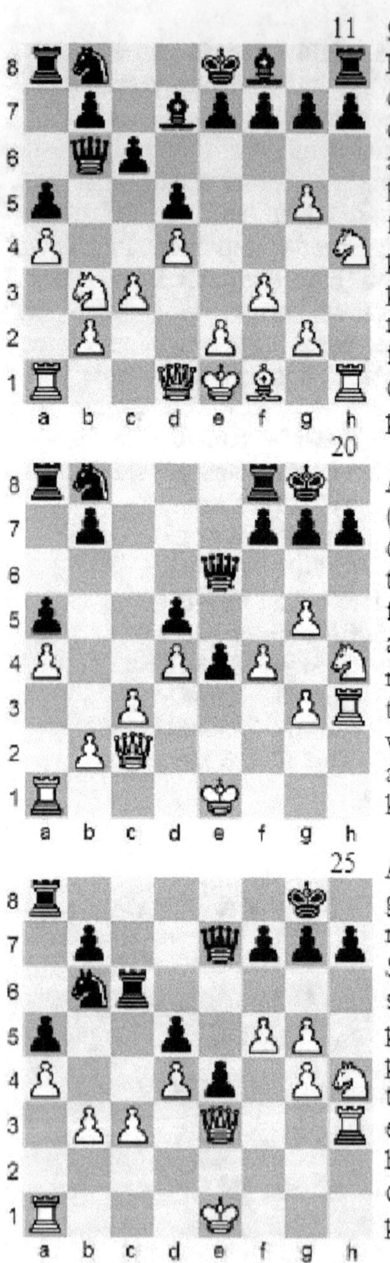

Summary

By cunning maneuvers on the queenside, White had distracted opponent's attention from his true attacking intention on kingside. He had developed quickly his pieces from queenside and had simulated preparation of long castling. To prevent this, Black had made moves that have not contributed to fast and harmonious development of minor pieces, as it should be played in opening (see Diag. 11).

After 20 moves from the beginning (see Diag. 20) Black has only the queen developed, while White has three pieces, all in good positions for future attack: the queen on c2 and the h3-rook – both ready to make a killer battery on h-file, and the h4-knight – ready to participate with f- and g- pawns at imminent and quick disorganization of black king's defense.

At only 25 moves of starting the game (see Diag. 25), White reached the *Moment of Effective Superiority* (MES). He cumulated small advantages obtained due to precise execution of own strategic plan and his position became able to support a final decisive coup to ensure the victory. This game highlights again great importance of a good strategic plan and of its precise and consequent execution.

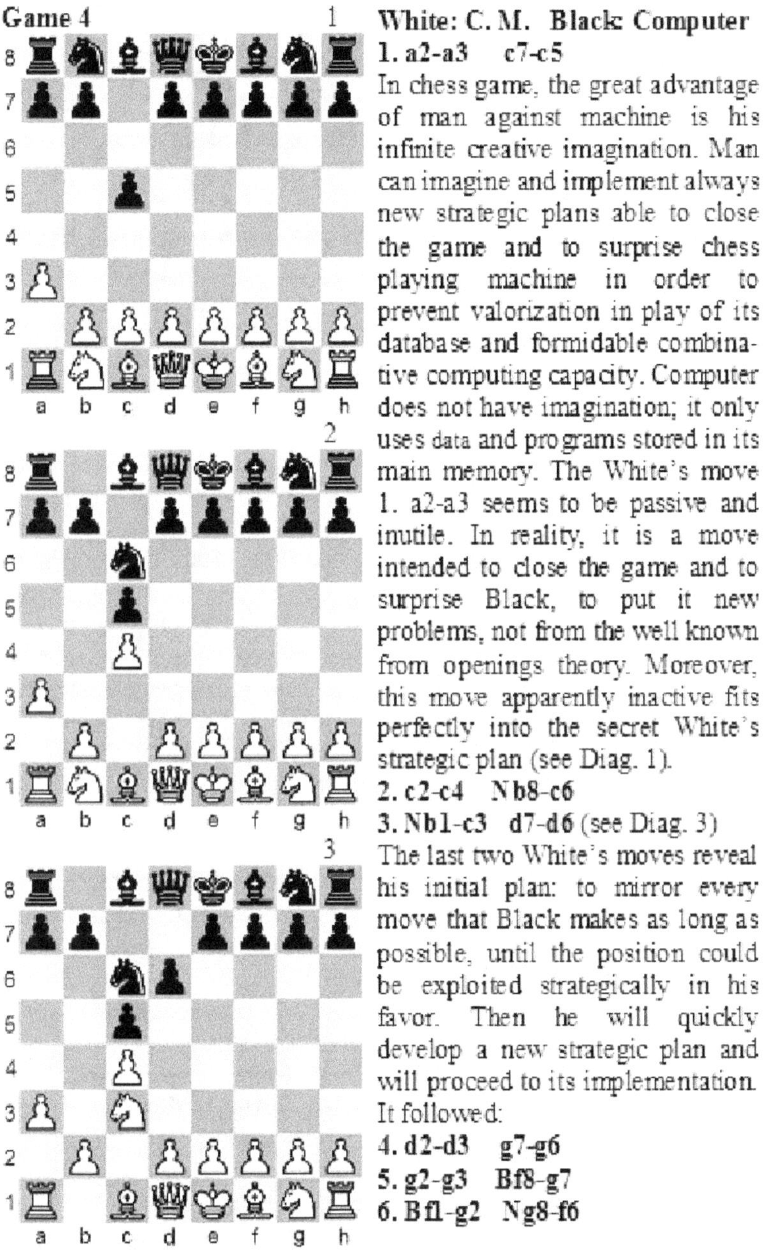

White: C. M. Black: Computer

1. a2-a3 c7-c5

In chess game, the great advantage of man against machine is his infinite creative imagination. Man can imagine and implement always new strategic plans able to close the game and to surprise chess playing machine in order to prevent valorization in play of its database and formidable combinative computing capacity. Computer does not have imagination; it only uses data and programs stored in its main memory. The White's move 1. a2-a3 seems to be passive and inutile. In reality, it is a move intended to close the game and to surprise Black, to put it new problems, not from the well known from openings theory. Moreover, this move apparently inactive fits perfectly into the secret White's strategic plan (see Diag. 1).

2. c2-c4 Nb8-c6

3. Nb1-c3 d7-d6 (see Diag. 3)

The last two White's moves reveal his initial plan: to mirror every move that Black makes as long as possible, until the position could be exploited strategically in his favor. Then he will quickly develop a new strategic plan and will proceed to its implementation. It followed:

4. d2-d3 g7-g6

5. g2-g3 Bf8-g7

6. Bf1-g2 Ng8-f6

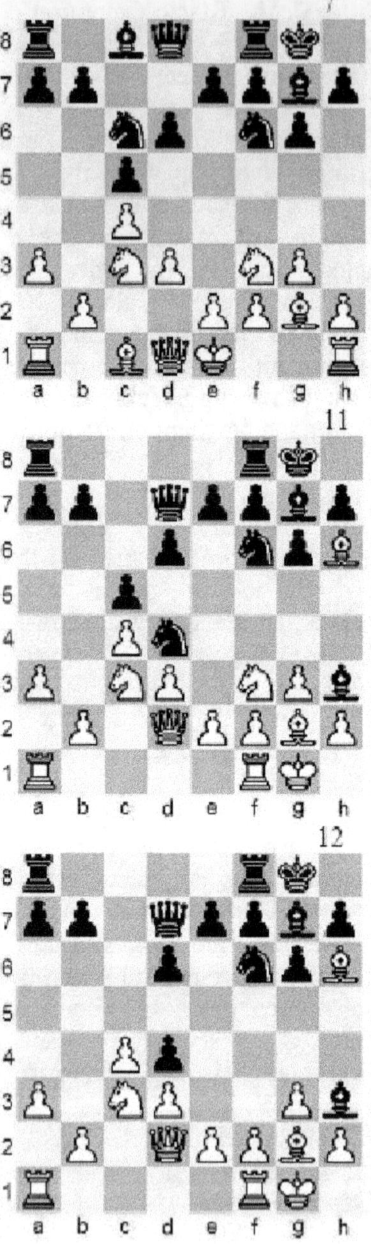

7. Ng1-f3 O-O (see Diag. 7)
8. O-O Bc8-g4
9. Bc1-g5 Qd8-d7
10. Qd1-d2 Bg4-h3
11. Bg5-h6 Nc6-d4 (see D. 11)

After this relatively quiet series of moves we can see that Black has a game plan which aims to quickly open the game in center by an attack with its three central pawns well supported by minor pieces. From the tactical point of view, so for a short term, this plan seems to be good and feasible if White will not find a solution to close again the game in center and on kingside. But from the strategic point of view, so for a long term, Black's plan leaves only two black pawns to face three white pawns on the queenside, position which may lead to a white protected passed pawn very dangerous in the endgame.

12. Nf3xd4! c5xd4

Unfortunately for Black, there is a solution to close again the game in center and on kingside and White will find and use it with accuracy. The White's move starts the fight to maintain center locked and to create a white pawn majority on first three files. In this regard the next sequence of moves is very instructive, both from the point of view strategic and tactical.

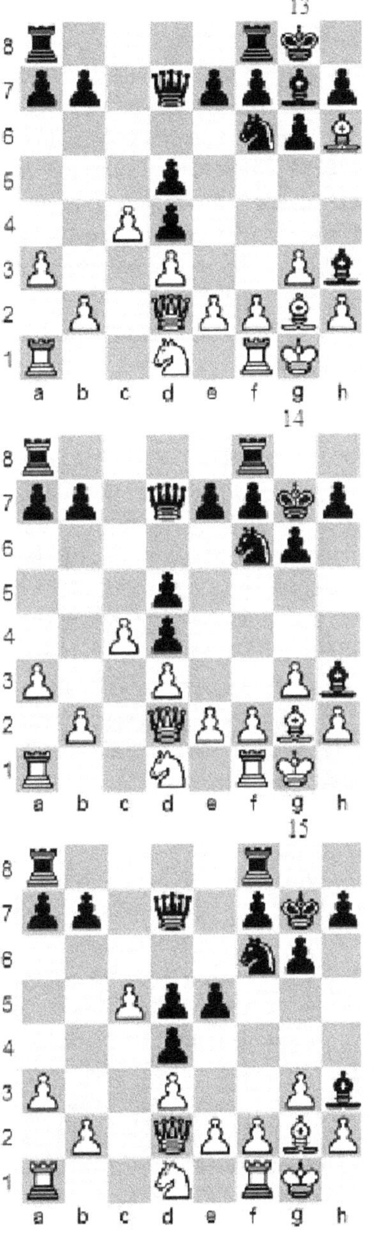

13. Nc3-d1! d6-d5
Black provides an exchange of pawns on d5. This exchange would be evidently favorable only for Black, because would open the game in center and would allow it employment of d5-square to transfer there its queen after the exchange of light-squared bishops on g2. In addition it would help eliminate one of the black double pawns from d-file.

14. Bh6xg7 Kg8xg7
White clearly made a strategic move that eliminates a piece from the defensive device of opponent's king and of dark squares around it. For this move he "has consumed" a minor piece for which still sees no other role in his plan of attack. In addition, he has exempted the queen from the task of defending h6-square, in order to make it free to play on queenside.

15. c4-c5! e7-e5
Again a White's strategic move, particularly important for the fate of the game. As we showed before at 13th move, the exchange of pawns on d5-square is not favorable for White. Therefore he refuses it and advances c-pawn to create a white pawn majority on queenside in accordance with his new strategic plan.

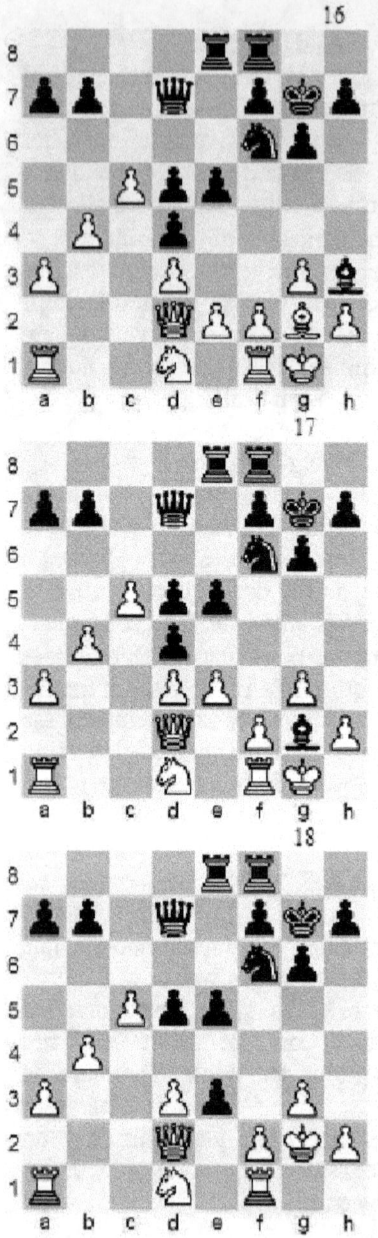

16. b2-b4 Ra8-e8

White pawns start to advance threateningly on queenside and Black understands that it will very hard or maybe even impossible to stop them. Therefore it prepares a counterattack in center on e4-square where it wants to offer a favorable pawn exchange, whose acceptance would create two very aggressive connected black pawns on d4 and e4.

17. e2-e3! Bh3xg2

Again a strategic White's move required by his plan execution and made at the right moment. It is the only move that still can block the advancement of black pawns in the center and the favorable for Black opening of the game. The white two connected pawns on d3 and e3 is an insurmountable barrier for the offensive two connected black pawns from the same files.

18. Kg1xg2 d4xe3

Black has nothing better to do. Therefore it decides just to exchange one of its two pawns from d-file and get two connected pawn on d- and e- files. But this move will not help it to open the game in center if White will choose the right move from the three possibilities to take the black pawn appeared on e3-square after the Black's move.

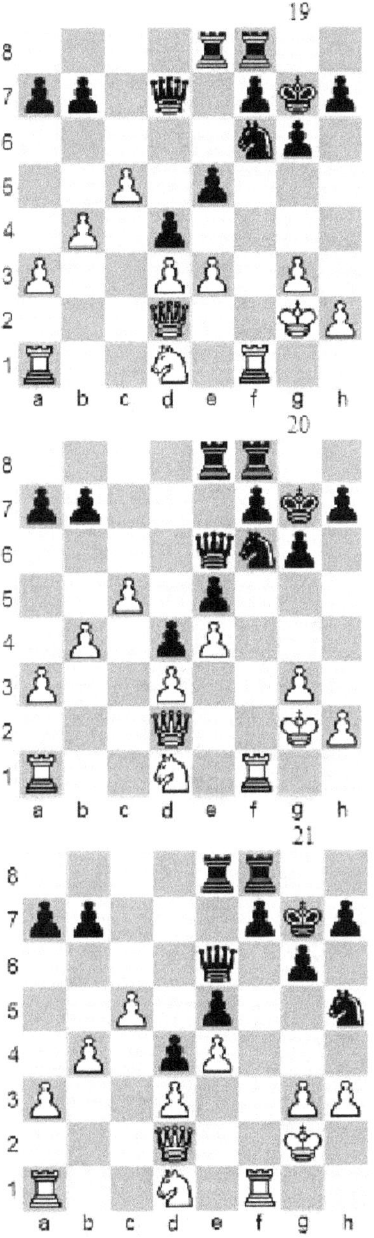

19. f2xe3! d5-d4

White chooses only strategically and tactically correct continuation: the move that recreates the strong barrier formed by two white connected pawns in front of attacking two black connected pawns on d- and e- files. In addition, he opens the f-file where can make a battery with his rooks to attack the black f7-pawn – the base of black king's defense.

20. e3-e4! Qd7-e6

White refuses again the exchange of pawns on d4-square offered by Black and closes definitively the game in center and on kingside, according to his strategic plan. Black wants to transfer its queen on b3 to create a pressure on queenside and to delay or even to stop from behind the dangerous advancement of White's pawns.

21. h2-h3! Nf6-h5

Before advancing of his pawns on queenside, White takes under control the g4-square to avoid black queen or knight to go there and to begin a counterattack supported by pawns against the white king. Also White prepares the move g3-g4 if Black will advance f-pawn on f4 trying to open the game and to create tactical complications on kingside.

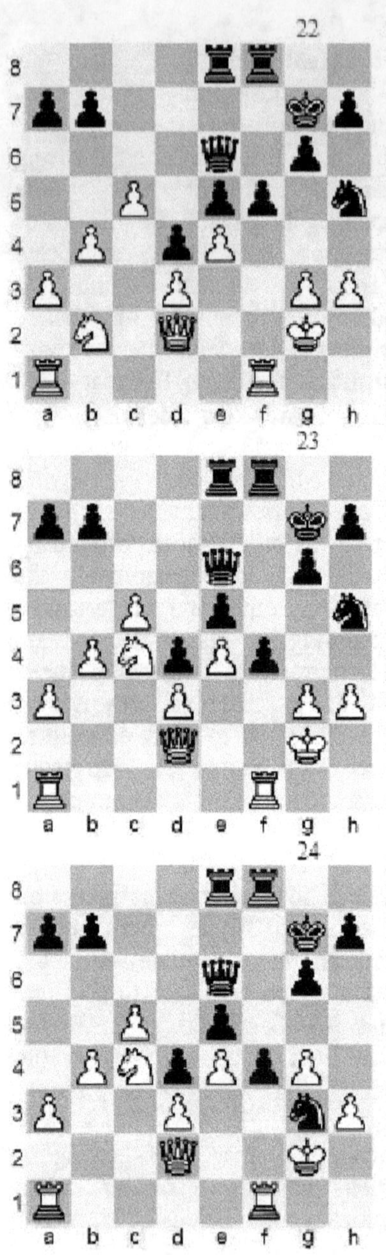

22. Nd1-b2 f7-f5

White wants to maximize the contribution of his knight in attack on queenside, where own strategic plan provides to be final battle for victory. Black correctly assessed that its salvation can come only through a successful attack on the kingside, where now White's position looks weaker after the disappearance of f2-pawn, base of the protective pawn chain of white king.

23. Nb2-c4 f5-f4

This time Black is who refuses the exchange of pawns on e4-squaare, correctly stating that it not enough would weaken the defense of white king. Indeed, after 23…fxe 24. dxe and 25.Nd3 center still remains blocked and Black's attack appears without clear perspectives of development and of real threats against its opponent.

24. g3-g4! Nh5-g3

Black has only partially achieved the goal: its knight has infiltrated the opponent's position and seems to have reached the maximum of power. In reality, black knight was completely isolated from the place where will be the final battle; now it has no possibility to help the other black pieces to stop the advancement of white pawns on queenside.

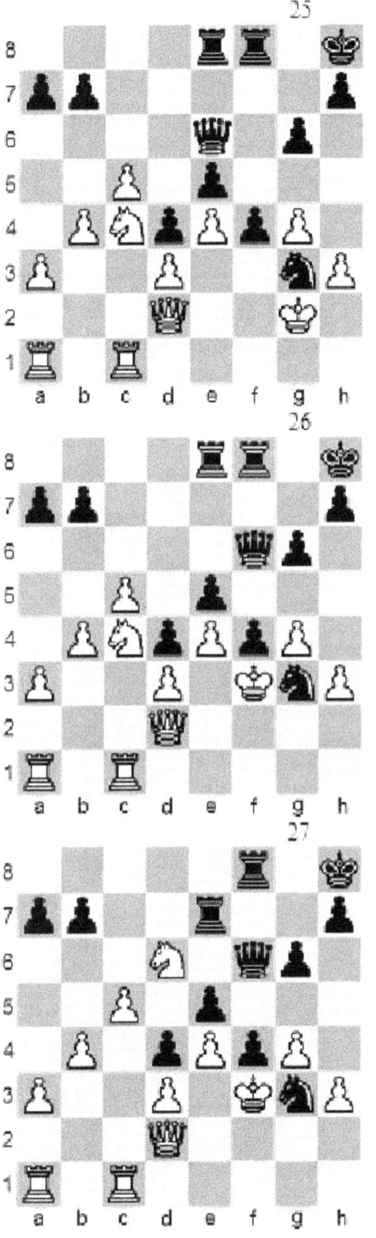

25. Rf1-c1 Kg7-h8

Bringing its knight on g3, Black has not created threats, so White begins to prepare the final attack. Starting with the move of rook on c1, all white pieces except the king are able to participate immediately in support of pawn advancement to the transformation on the 8th rank. Black intends to bring f8-rook on g8-square to begin a counterattack against white king.

26. Kg2-f3! Qe6-f6

White king participates itself in its defense blocking black f4-pawn to advance and create threats that need defensive tasks for white pieces. More, white king uses black f4-pawn as if it would be a white protective pawn, a part of White's defending device. An instructive practical example of use of an opponent's piece in our plan achievement as an own piece.

27. Nc4-d6 Re8-e7

White knight attacks the b7-pawn and occupies a central square from which it creates multiple threats and encumbers black pieces to collaborate in defense. White reached the *Moment of Effective Superiority* (MES - see Ch. 4). On queenside he has more pawns and pieces than Black and a better position that ensures his victory.

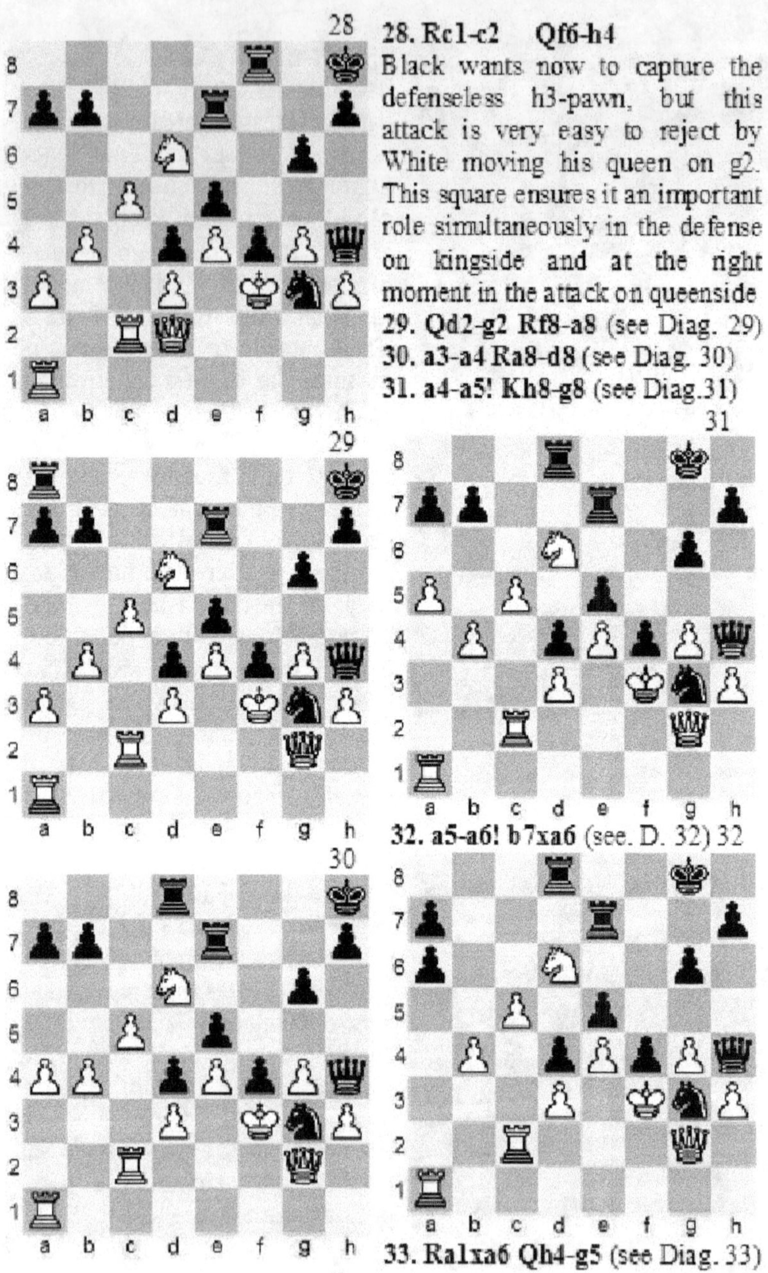

28. Rc1-c2 Qf6-h4

Black wants now to capture the defenseless h3-pawn, but this attack is very easy to reject by White moving his queen on g2. This square ensures it an important role simultaneously in the defense on kingside and at the right moment in the attack on queenside

29. Qd2-g2 Rf8-a8 (see Diag. 29)

30. a3-a4 Ra8-d8 (see Diag. 30)

31. a4-a5! Kh8-g8 (see Diag.31)

32. a5-a6! b7xa6 (see. D. 32)

33. Ra1xa6 Qh4-g5 (see Diag. 33)

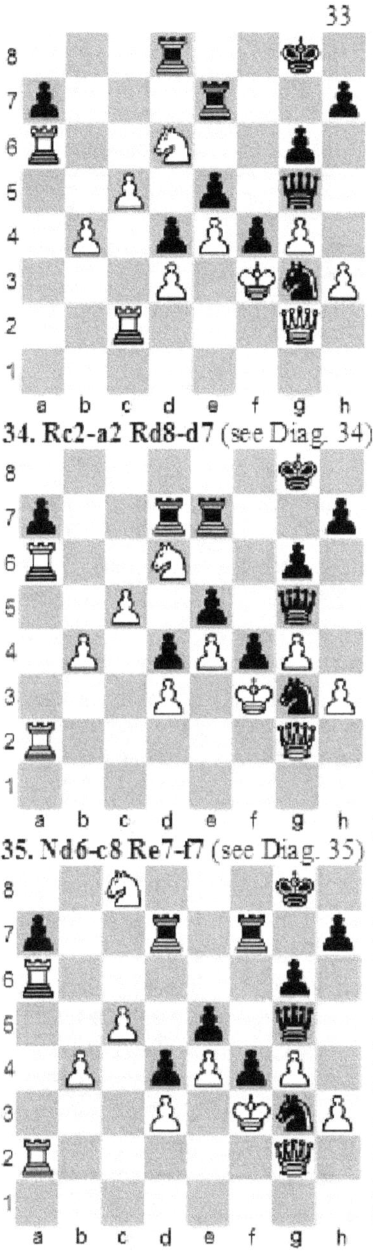

33

34. Rc2-a2 Rd8-d7 (see Diag. 34)

35. Nd6-c8 Re7-f7 (see Diag. 35)

36. Nc8xa7 and White wins.

The advancement of white passed pawns on queenside cannot be stopped and Black does not have enough time or a position that would allow it a kingside counter-attack. (see Diag. 36).

36

Summary

White began the game with a very unusual move and then played "mirror" to surprise the opponent. Playing without a plan or model stored in memory, at 11th move Black has committed a small strategic error that allows White to develop a new plan to win. Then, playing move by move according to the method explained in the second part of this book, White has won in a very instructive manner. Each White's move had an active quadruple strategic-tactical and defensive-offensive character. This allowed him to gain easily some positional advantages that summed have ensured his victory.

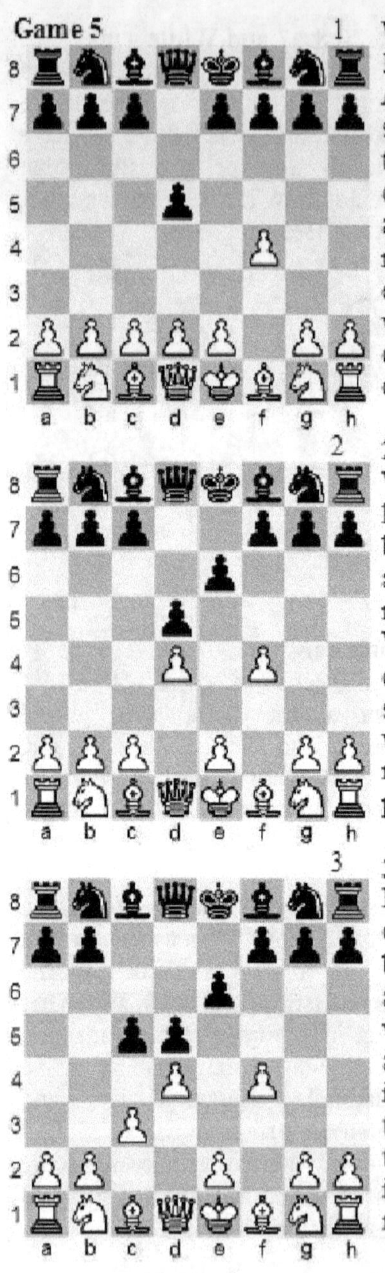

White: C. M. Black: Computer

1. f2-f4! d7-d5

As in previous games, in his strategic plan, even starting with the first move, White seeks rapidly closing the game and delaying activation of black pieces, by all means. One of this means is the exchange of pawns or pieces, which must be offered or accepted only if it is clearly favorable for our plan, as in this game.

2. d2-d4! e7-e6

With his move, White blocks for long time the opening of the game by move e7-e5. Also Black's attempt with the same goal by the move c7-c5 will also fail, because White will not accept the exchange of pawns on c5-square, but on d4-square, and only after its defense with the move e2-e3 that ensures replacement of exchanged d4-pawn.

3. c2-c3 c7-c5

In chess game, victory can be obtained easier if even from the beginning we prepare a decisive attack on one side, depending on what our opponent plays, based on a strategic plan set out commonly in advance. White over-defends the d4-pawn and allows his queen to move on c2, where it does not impede the rapid development of minor pieces and the castling.

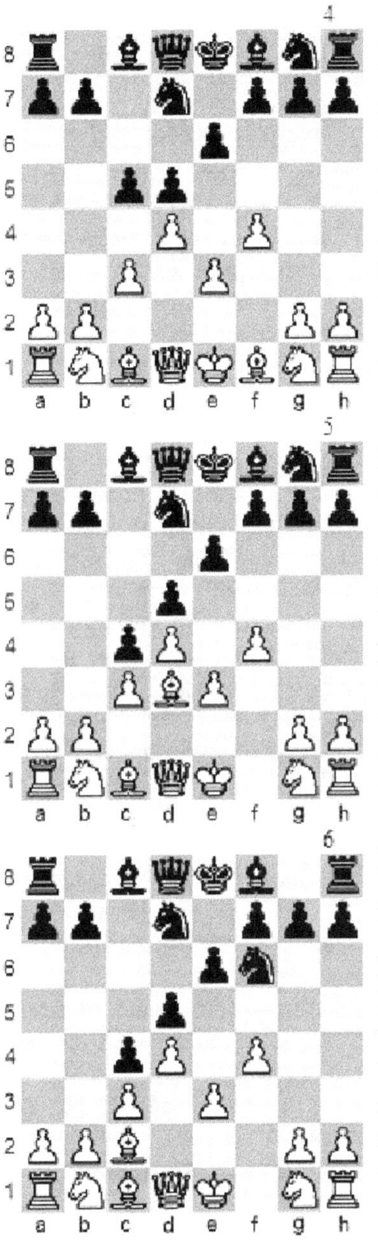

4. e2-e3! Nb8-d7

White makes accurately the best move that corresponds to his strategic plan. Black brings knight from b8 to d7 to take place of black pawn after it exchange on c5 and thus to get there a good active position. But White refuses the proposed pawn exchange on c5 and continues pieces development according to the strategic plan.

5. Bf1-d3! c5-c4

Knowing Black's preference to attack any opponent's piece as soon as it could, White makes a cunning move which invites it to attack the light-squared white bishop intentionally brought on d3. Black falls into this trap and without intention consumes a tempo and a pawn in order to contribute to achievement of opponent's strategic plan.

6. Bd3-c2 Ng8-f6

White bishop remains active on the important diagonal b1-h7. At first glance, the position seems to be preferable for Black, because it has two minor pieces developed, while White has only one. In reality, White's position is potentially much better prepared for a rapid attack on kingside, as you will see after a couple of moves.

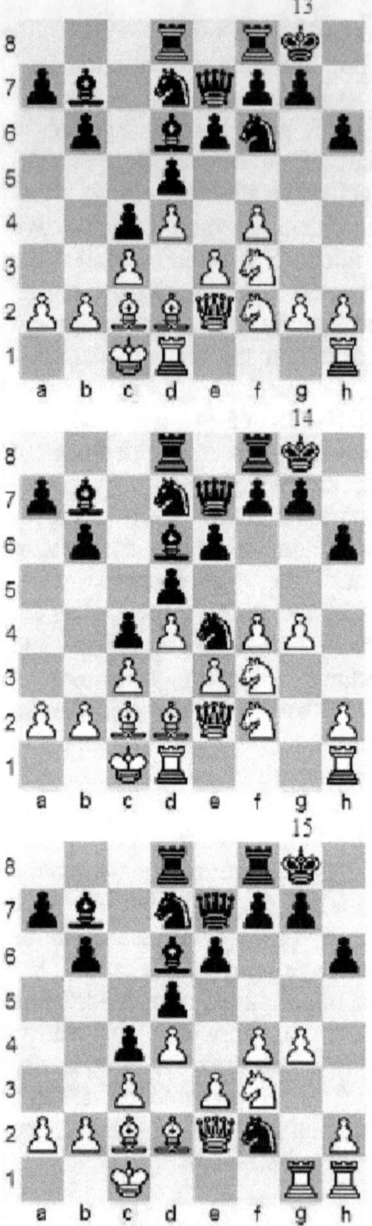

Until the position of Diag. 13 were performed following moves: 7. **Nb1-d2 Bf8-d6 8. Nd2-f3! Qd8-e7 9. Ng1-h3! b7-b6 10. Nh3-f2 Nc8-b7 11. Qd1-e2 h7-h6 12. Bc1-d2 O-O 13. O-O-O Ra8-d8.** Al White's pieces are placed for an active and quick participation in attack against defensive device of opponent's king. Black seems to not anticipate the danger.

14. g2-g4! Nf6-e4

White g-pawn already start attack, well defended and supported by all pieces, except the king. Now Black notifies that White can mobilize quickly more pieces in attack than can it bring in defense. So as to decrease the pressure being put on its kingside defense, Black decides to exchange the f6-knight for one of white pieces which can support the advancement of white pawns.

15. Rd1-g1! Ne4xf2

White does not accept exchange of knights on e4-square, because after that his f3-knight must retire back, thereby losing an excellent square for starting in attack and impeding movement of other white pieces. He continues the mobilization of pieces in attack and accepts the exchange of knights on f2-square because thus brings his queen on a better position.

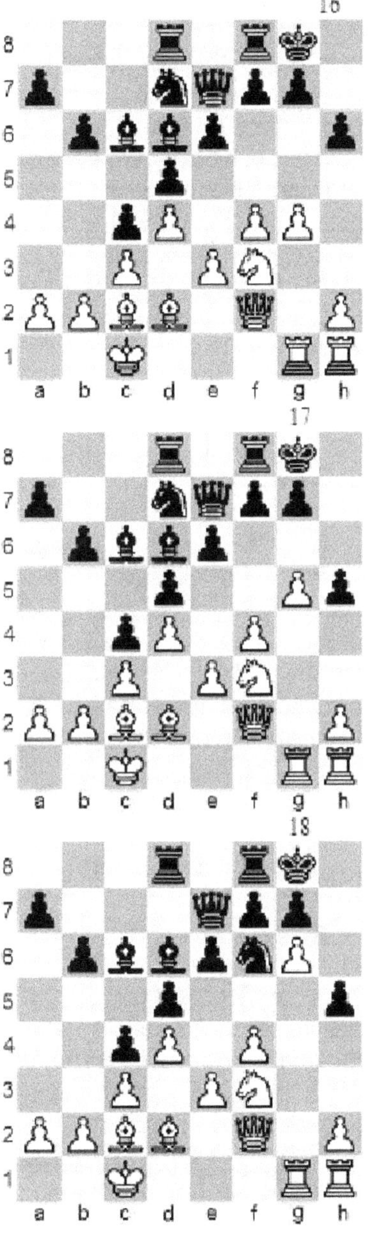

16. Qe2xf2 Bb7-c6
Black anticipates the great force of White's attack on kingside and decides to bring in defense the inactive b7-bishop through c6- and f8- squares. But for this maneuver Black must lose two very precious tempos which will be used by White to increase the pressure advancing g4-pawn twice to break the black pawn defensive devise.

17. g4-g5! h6-h5
White offers a favorable exchange of pawns on g5-square. If Black accepts it, the g-file will be open and after17...h6xg5 18. Rg1xg5 all white pieces can attack with increased power the black king and end of game will come soon. Black avoids the exchange and advances the attacked pawn on h5 where it is not yet in danger.

18. g5-g6! Nd7-f6
White immediately occupies g6-square where Black hopes to move the g7-pawn to defend the h5-pawn and to slow temporarily the opponent's attack. Now, if Black refuses the exchange of pawns on g6, then the black h5-pawn becomes an easy prey for white pieces ready to capture it. Black makes a last attempt to defend this isolated pawn.

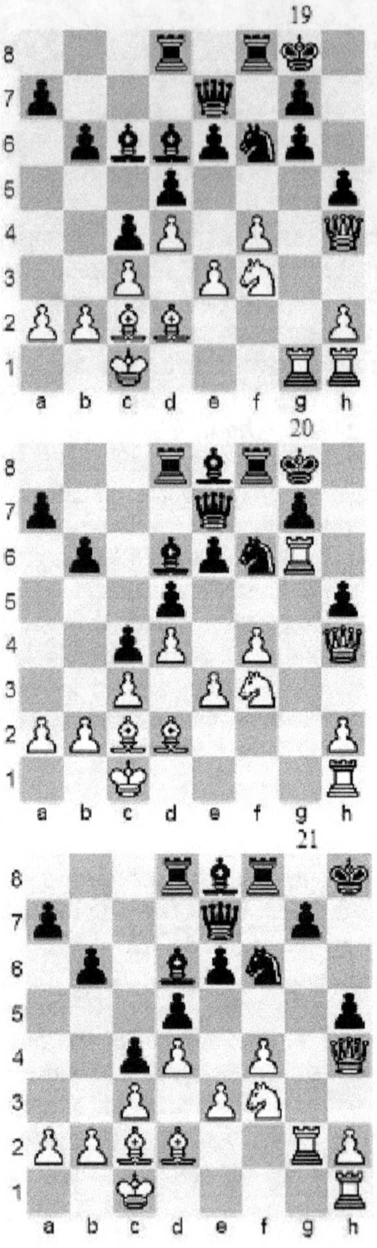

19. Qf2-h4! f7xg6
White begins the attack on h5-pawn. Directly or indirectly, he can contribute to this attack with all pieces except the dark-squared bishop and the king, so with five pieces. Black can defend quickly h5-square only with four pieces: f7-pawn, f6-knight, c6-bishop and f8-rook, so the h5-pawn cannot be defended.

20. Rg1xg6 Bc6-e8
Black is forced to accept the exchange of pawns on g6, because only in this way it will be able to use the c6-bishop to defend h5-pawn from e8-square. But unfortunately for Black, this exchange opens the g-file for the battery of the two white rooks and will create new threats which will make impossible a sufficient defense of black king.

21. Rg6-g2 Kg8-h8
White prepares now a battery of rooks on g-file, having as target the weak black g7-pawn. This new threat forced Black to clear the way for the f8-rook's move on g8 to defend the g7-pawn. But when White will terminate to place pieces in attack of both h5 and g7 two weaknesses, Black will not have sufficient resources to defend them simultaneously.

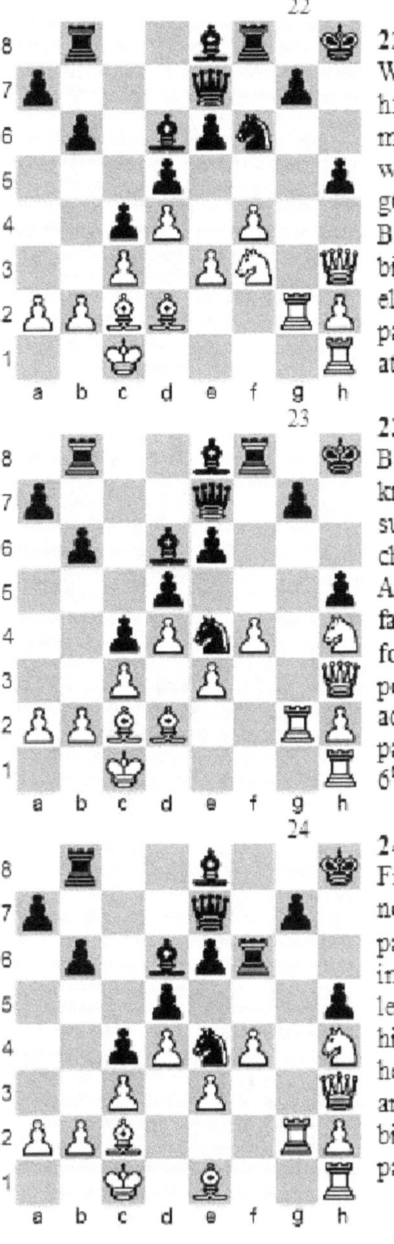

22. Qh4-h3 Rd8-b8
White queen continues to attack h5-pawn, but withdraws a step to make clear way for passing of white knight from f3 through h4 to g6-square where he will force Black to accept it exchange for e8-bishop. In this way White will eliminate the main defender of h5-pawn. Black hopes to have time to attack on queenside.

23. Nf3-h4 Nf6-e4
Black intends to exchange its knight for white d2-bishop – the support of the defensive pawn chain that protects white king. Also, on e4-square it offers a favorable exchange of black knight for the white c2-bishop, one of the potential attackers of h5-pawn. In addition, Black allows f8-rook to participate in its king defense on 6th and 7th ranks.

24. Bd2-e1! Rf8-f6
From the e4-square black knight no longer defends the weak h5-pawn and no threats something immediately, so that White can leave it where it is and keep both his bishops for attack. Therefore, he refuses both exchanges on e4 and d2 and moves dark-squared bishop on e1 from where it can participate better in attack.

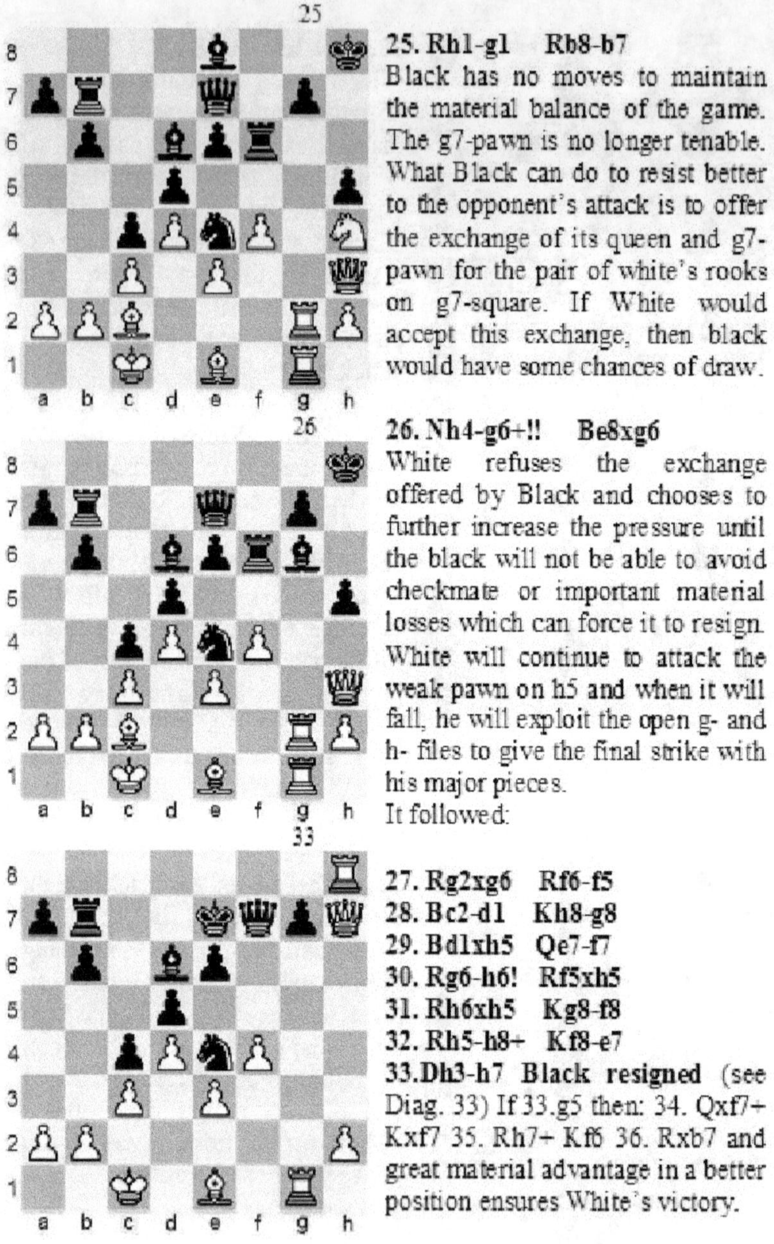

25. Rh1-g1 Rb8-b7
Black has no moves to maintain the material balance of the game. The g7-pawn is no longer tenable. What Black can do to resist better to the opponent's attack is to offer the exchange of its queen and g7-pawn for the pair of white's rooks on g7-square. If White would accept this exchange, then black would have some chances of draw.

26. Nh4-g6+!! Be8xg6
White refuses the exchange offered by Black and chooses to further increase the pressure until the black will not be able to avoid checkmate or important material losses which can force it to resign. White will continue to attack the weak pawn on h5 and when it will fall, he will exploit the open g- and h- files to give the final strike with his major pieces.
It followed:

27. Rg2xg6 Rf6-f5
28. Bc2-d1 Kh8-g8
29. Bd1xh5 Qe7-f7
30. Rg6-h6! Rf5xh5
31. Rh6xh5 Kg8-f8
32. Rh5-h8+ Kf8-e7
33.Dh3-h7 Black resigned (see Diag. 33) If 33.g5 then: 34. Qxf7+ Kxf7 35. Rh7+ Kf6 36. Rxb7 and great material advantage in a better position ensures White's victory.

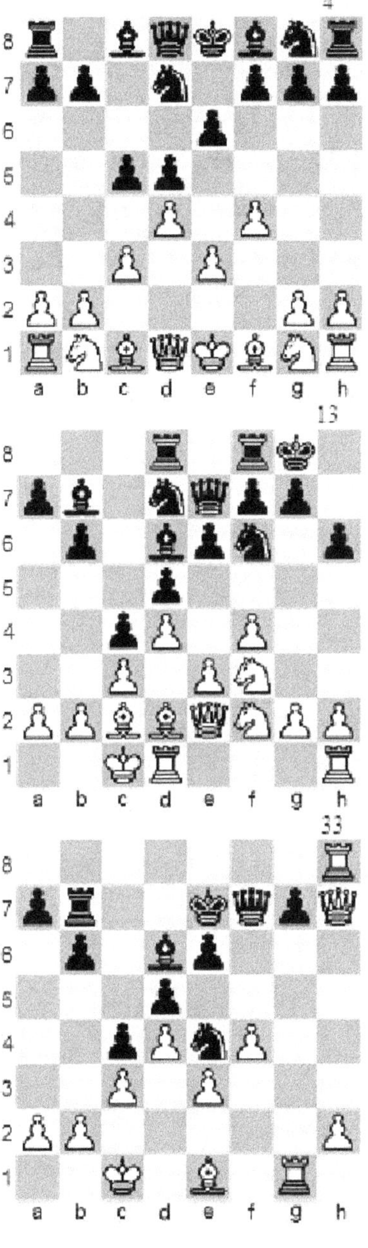

Summary

Scientific systemic vision of organization and management of chess play forms in player's brain the habit of seeing the game as a whole, and which runs from the first move according to a strategic plan established commonly in advance. Moves get a quadruple character (offensive-defensive and strategic-tactical), coherence and an increased force. Playing under scientific systemic requirements of player thinking organization and management, presented in 2th part of this book, all available chess resources can be used much more efficiently. Learning all these new knowledge requires a minimum effort, but it is fully rewarded later during games because winning moves can be found much more easily. The player "reads" correctly position and knows precisely what to do, how, when and where. In this 5th game, through first four moves made in an order previously established, White creates a pawn chain designed to close the game in center and on queenside in order to allow a calm and thorough preparation of a powerful attack on the other side if Black will castle there (see Diag. 4). After nine moves this preparation was completed (see Diag. 13). It followed a vigorous attack and the result can be seen in Diag. 33.

This game clearly illustrates the basic strategic plan, also successfully used by author in previous games, and suggests the great importance of using a scientific strategic plan developed and applied consequently and accurately, plan that links moves in a logical continuous chain and focuses their effects both in defense and especially in successful preparation and development of the decisive attack.

9. Summary

In this book are first analyzed and redefined in a systemic vision all fundamental concepts relating to organization and management on a scientific basis of complex human activities, including business activities and strategic games.

Redefinition has been made under a law of nature which was discovered recently by the author: **the Universal Law of Organization**, represented graphically by **the Universal Model of Organization and Management** (Fig. 1).

How can practically be used this law of nature to improve the managerial decisions it shows into a final didactic study of thinking in chess game, with examples of games played against the computer, almost move-by-move presented by commented chess diagrams.

This detailed and pictured mode of presentation allows profound understanding of the game, both as a whole and in detail, and how to play simultaneously for fulfillment of a strategic plan and for tactical kicks, using only moves with quadruple character (defensive-offensive and strategic-tactical).

The book is written so as to be easy reading for all. Every game is presented as a story, like a chain of interesting events, and so the reader to be able to fully enjoy the unique beauty of this marvelous game of imagination and intelligence.

Traditional management, developed empirically and based only on observations from practical experience, it's time to be replaced by scientific management, based on *systemics* and *cybernetics.* Success is guaranteed if the business is organized and managed as an adaptable cybernetic system on the scientific basis of this book.

Today, more than ever before, to obtain high performance in chess as in business, it takes a systemic approach to solve the complex problems of organization and management.

In short, studying this book, readers can find out how quickly and accurately can build and drive systems necessary to achieve their objectives and how to train imagination and intelligence for this purpose.

This book appears both in pocket printed format and in digital format on DVD or online.

10. Bibliography

1. Taylor, Frederick Winslow, *The Principles of Scientific Management*, New York, 1911;

2. Fayol, H., *Administration industrielle et générale,* Dunod, Paris, 1916 ;

3. Mihăescu C., *The Universal Law of Organization*, în *Proceedings I of The Fourth International Conference on Business Excellence,* 16-17 October 2009, Braşov, România / ed. Constantin Brătianu, Dorin Lixăndroiu, Nicolae Al. Pop – Braşov: Infomarket, 2009, p. 290.

4. Nicolescu O., *Noutăţi în managementul internaţional*, Editura Tehnică, Bucureşti, 1993, p. 18.

5. Mihăescu C., *Şah şi cibernetică,* Editura Sport-Turism, Bucureşti, 1986.

6. Mihăescu C., *L'utilisation de la conception systémique dans la projection des sous-systèmes informatiques servant a la direction des activités dans les entreprises,* în Proceedings I of the International Symposium on Applications of Mathematics in System

Theory, 27-30 Dec. 1978, Transilvania University of Brasov, Romania, p. 111.

7. Mihăescu C., *Noţiunile de "organizare" şi "conducere" în viziune sistemică*, în Revista Economică, nr. 49, Bucureşti, 1980, p. 20.

8. Mihaescu C., *Critical Success Factors in Organization and Management*, CreateSpace, USA, 2013.

9. Mihăescu C., *Afaceri mici şi mijlocii - Curs management ştiinţific*, CreateSpace, USA, 2014.

10. Mihăescu C., *Curs de şah şi management ştiinţific*, CreateSpace, USA, 2014.

To your success

Constantin Mihăescu

ctinmihaescu@gmail.com

11. About the Author

Constantin V. Mihaescu is a Romanian mechanical engineer, manager, management consulting expert, informaticien, scientific researcher and writer. After a long research and many experiments he has discovered a law of nature: the *Universal Law of Organization* – graphically represented by the *Universal Model of Organization and Management.* This model can be used to organize and manage in systemic scientific vision all human complex activities, to ensure maximum efficiency. He is invited member of the International Society for Performance Improvement (ISPI). One of the research themes approached was the application of *systemic scientific organization and management* for creative and innovative thinking improvement. As a result of this research, he wrote the book *Şah şi cibernetică* (Chess and Cybernetics) - an ample *scientific chess manual.* He was qualified in a semifinal of the Romanian National Chess Championship, competition in that he has successfully tested many of his own original concepts presented in this book. He has published nonfiction books, articles, short stories and science fiction.

www.ingramcontent.com/pod-product-compliance
Lightning Source LLC
Chambersburg PA
CBHW070809180526
45168CB00002B/552

* 9 7 8 1 5 1 5 0 3 4 1 4 8 *